**Barnabas**
for
Children®

Barnabas for Children® is a registered word mark
and the logo is a registered device mark
of The Bible Reading Fellowship.

Published by
The Bible Reading Fellowship
15 The Chambers, Vineyard
Abingdon OX14 3FE, United Kingdom
Tel: +44 (0)1865 319700
Email: enquiries@brf.org.uk; Website: www.brf.org.uk
BRF is a Registered Charity

ISBN 978 0 85746 354 8
First published 2007
This edition first published 2015

Copyright © 2007 Anno Domini Publishing
www.ad-publishing.com
Text copyright © 2007 Rhona Davies
Illustrations copyright © 2007 Marcin Piwowarski

Publishing Director Annette Reynolds
Consulting Editor Jenny Hyatt
Art Director Gerald Rogers
Pre-production Krystyna Kowalska Hewitt

Printed and bound in Singapore

THE BARNABAS
PAGE A DAY
BIBLE

Rhona Davies
Illustrated by Marcin Piwowarski

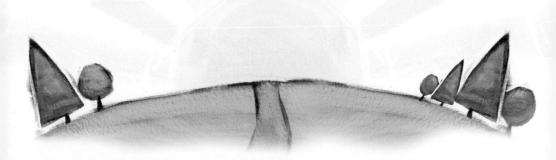

CONTENTS

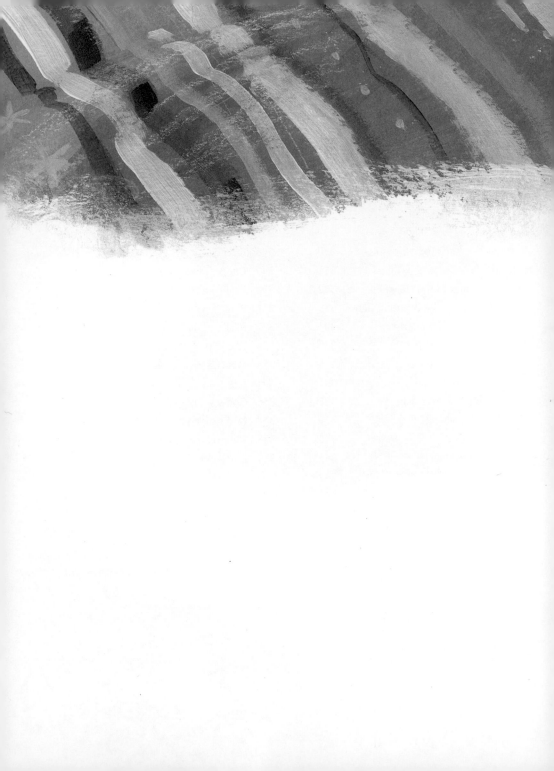

THE OLD TESTAMENT

1 IN THE BEGINNING

In the beginning there was nothing. It was dark and empty and shapeless.

'Let there be light!' God said. As soon as he had said the words, light came into existence. God saw that the light was good. God divided the light, so that there was day and there was night.

God made the sky and separated it from the waters below.

God made the seas and created dry land.

'Let the land produce plants and trees full of seeds and fruits,' God said. Then every variety of green and leafy vegetation filled the land, from tall redwood trees to olives and oranges, acorns and chestnuts. God saw that all he had made was good.

'Let there be lights in the sky to mark night and day, times and seasons, months and years,' God said. So the golden sun shone in the day and the silvery moon beamed in the night sky. God saw that all he had made was good.

'Let the waters be filled with living creatures and the skies with birds. Let them multiply and increase in number.' Then there were dolphins and sea horses, eagles, owls, robins and wrens, buzzing bees and beautiful butterflies.

'Let the land be filled with creatures,' God said. So there were sheep, goats, elephants, giraffe, lions, tigers and graceful gazelles.

God looked at what he had made and saw that it was good.

Then God made man and woman. He put them in charge of his creation, to care for it and cultivate it for food. God loved the people he had made and he saw that everything he had made was very good. Then God rested.

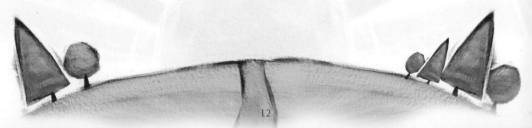

2 THE PERFECT WORLD

God gave Adam and Eve a beautiful garden to live in. It was full of
plants and trees with fruit they could eat. The garden was watered by
a river that ran through it, and Adam and Eve tended the garden and
worked in it.

Adam and Eve were good company for each other. They shared
the work and they lived happily together. Adam gave names to all the
creatures that God had made.

God told them that they could eat anything that grew in the garden
except the fruit of one tree in the middle of the garden, the tree of the
knowledge of good and evil.

3 RIGHT AND WRONG

One of the creatures in the garden was a snake.

He came to Eve and tempted her.

'Did God really tell you not to eat from any of the trees in the garden?' he asked.

'God told us we can eat from every tree, except the tree in the middle of the garden,' said Eve. 'If we eat from that tree, we will die.'

'You will not die…' said the snake. 'God does not want you to eat from that tree because if you do, you will know good and evil just as God does.'

Eve looked at the tree. She saw how lovely its fruit looked and thought about what the snake had said. She took some of the fruit and ate it. Then she gave it to Adam and he ate some too.

As soon as they had eaten, Adam and Eve knew what they had done. They realised why God had told them not to eat the fruit. Now they had disobeyed God and it was too late to put things right. They felt guilty and ashamed and when they heard God coming in the garden, they found trees to hide among so he would not see them.

4 ADAM AND EVE ARE SENT AWAY

God called out to Adam.

'Where are you?'

'I was afraid, so I hid,' replied Adam.

'Have you then eaten from the tree of the knowledge of good and evil?' God asked.

'It wasn't my fault,' said Adam. 'The woman gave it to me to eat.'

'What have you done?' God asked Eve.

'It wasn't my fault,' said Eve. 'The snake tricked me and I ate the fruit.'

God was very sad. He turned to the snake and told it that it would crawl on its belly from that time on. He turned to Eve and told her that she would have pain as she gave birth to her children. He told Adam that thorns and thistles would choke the plants he grew.

Then God banished Adam and Eve from the garden he had given them. They had chosen to disobey him. They now knew the difference between what was right and what was wrong. They would know suffering and death; they could not be God's friends any more.

5 CAIN AND ABEL

After a time Eve gave birth to two sons, Cain and Abel.

Both boys grew up to be farmers. They knew how much they depended on God to give them sun and rain for the harvests and to help their animals give birth to healthy lambs and kids. Cain planted seeds and grew crops while Abel kept the sheep and goats.

One day, Cain brought some of his crops as a gift to God, to thank him for the harvest. Abel also brought a gift of the first of his newborn lambs. God saw not only the gift that was brought but the two brothers. He knew that Abel had brought his gift out of faith, because he loved God. God also knew that Cain had brought his gift because he thought he had to, not because he cared about God. God was pleased with Abel, but he was disappointed with Cain. And Cain knew it.

'Why are you angry, Cain?' asked God. 'Do what is right and you will be accepted. Beware of your bad temper. Don't let it control you or it may destroy you.'

Cain knew that God was right, but he wouldn't listen. He could think of nothing except having revenge on his brother.

Cain asked Abel to go out into the field with him; he planned to wait for the right moment and kill him there.

Later God asked Cain where his brother was.

'How should I know?' lied Cain. 'Is it my job to look after him?'

'I warned you about your anger,' said God. 'Now your brother's death is on your conscience. You will know what it is to feel guilt for your wrongdoing.'

God was good to Adam and Eve. He gave them another son, Seth, because Cain had killed his brother, and then other sons and daughters.

6 NOAH'S ARK

Many years passed and the land became full of people. Few remembered who God was. They did as they pleased. They took what they wanted from others. They spoiled the world that God had made and thought only of themselves. God knew that the world had become an evil place, full of greed, hatred and violence. He decided to wash it clean and start all over again.

There was one man who remembered God. His name was Noah. Noah had a wife and three sons, Shem, Ham and Japheth.

'Noah!' God said one day. 'I am going to end all the evil there is in the world. I want you to build an ark—a huge boat that will float on the flood waters that I will send to wash the earth clean. I will tell you exactly how to build it so that you and your family and two of every kind of creature will be safe inside the ark.'

God told Noah how to build the ark. He told him how long it was to be, how many decks it should have, and where to put the door. God told Noah to coat the ark with pitch to keep the water out, and to fill it with supplies of food.

Noah set about building the ark. He began to make the huge boat miles from any sea. It took him many years of his life; and the people around him watched and thought he was mad.

7 THE GREAT FLOOD

The ark was ready.

God told Noah to collect two of every kind of living creature, seven pairs of every kind of bird, and seven pairs of every animal that would be used for sacrifice. The animals came to Noah as if they too knew what God had planned, and Noah took them all on board the ark. Then God shut the door.

Outside the rain began to fall. The rain fell steadily until the streams and rivers were full and burst their banks; the rain fell until underground springs broke through the earth; the rain fell until no dry land could be seen anywhere around.

Everything that had lived upon the earth was destroyed by the flood. The ark that God had told Noah to build floated on the waters. God kept Noah, his family and all the animals safe inside the ark.

8 THE RAINBOW

Inside the ark, Noah, his wife, his three sons and their wives worked to care for the animals. Days passed. Weeks passed, and still the rain fell down.

Then one day it stopped. The ark floated gently.

Slowly, very slowly, the waters began to go down. The ark rested on the Ararat mountains. More weeks passed and the tops of the mountains became visible.

Then Noah took hold of a raven and set it free in the air. The bird stretched its wings and flew, but there was nowhere for it to land. It flew back and forth until there was food for it to find on the earth.

Noah waited a little longer, then he sent out a dove, to see if the land was yet dry. Water still covered the ground. The dove returned to the ark.

After seven days, Noah sent out the dove again. This time the bird returned with an olive leaf. Noah knew that the waters were going down.

Another seven days passed, and Noah sent out the dove for the third time. When the bird did not return, Noah knew that it had found somewhere to rest. Noah waited until God told him it was time to leave the ark.

Then they came out, Noah, his family and all the creatures that had been kept safe.

Noah watched as all the animals went to find their homes on the earth. Then he built an altar and sacrificed some of the birds he had brought for that purpose. Noah thanked God for keeping them all safe.

'I will never destroy all the earth with water again,' promised God. 'I have put a rainbow in the sky, as a sign of my promise.'

9 THE TOWER OF BABEL

Noah's sons had children of their own. Their families went on to have families too, and soon people spread out again across the land.

One of Ham's descendants was Nimrod. He was a mighty hunter and founded the city of Nineveh.

At that time everyone spoke the same language. They started to build not with stones, but with bricks baked in the hot sun. First they built cities; then one group of people decided to build a tower. The tower reached high into the sky so that everyone would see how great they were.

God saw the people as they were building the tower. He saw that once more they thought they were great and powerful and did not need him. God saw that they were proud and soon would be just like the people who had lived before the flood.

So God caused their language to be confused; now they couldn't understand each other.

The tower was abandoned and the people began to make new groups of people who each shared the same language.

God then scattered them further over all the earth.

10 TERAH'S JOURNEY

One of Shem's descendants was called Terah, who had three sons, Abram, Nahor and Haran. Terah did not worship God, but, like the people around him, worshipped a moon-god.

Haran, Terah's son, had a son called Lot, but then Haran died.

Nahor married Milcah and gave Terah grandchildren.

Abram married Sarai, but though they wanted a family very much, they did not have any children.

They all lived in the prosperous city of Ur of the Chaldeans until one day, Terah decided to move.

He left behind Nahor and his family, but took Abram and Sarai, and his grandson, Lot. They planned to travel to the land of Canaan, but on the way they stopped and made their home in a place called Haran.

Terah never left there. He died many years later, having never reached Canaan.

11 THE PROMISED LAND

God had chosen Abram even before his father moved to Haran. God had spoken to Abram while he still lived in Ur. God wanted to take him to Canaan, the land where he would set his people apart from other nations, and make of them a people who loved him and knew how to live the way he intended all people to live.

'You must leave here,' God had said to Abram. 'I will show you where you must go. I am going to make your family into a great nation.'

Abram did as God had told him. He packed up his possessions, prepared his servants, and took with him his wife, Sarai, and his nephew Lot.

They travelled together through the land, pitching their tents and moving on until they reached Canaan. Then God spoke to Abram again.

'This is the land I have promised to give to you and your children,' he said.

Abram built an altar there and thanked God. He believed God's promise, even though there were other people already living in Canaan.

12 LOT'S CHOICE

As time passed it became clear that Abram and Lot needed to choose different parts of the land in which to make their home. They each had many sheep and goats, oxen and camels. They each had many tents and servants.

Both men had become wealthy in possessions. The land did not have enough water for them all to enjoy and the servants started to quarrel.

'Let's not argue,' said Abram to Lot. 'We have this whole land to live in. Choose where you want to live, and I will take my family somewhere else.'

Lot looked about him. He saw that the plain before him was green and fertile. There was plenty of water. It would be a good place to live.

'I am happy to live in the Jordan valley,' Lot said. So the men parted. Lot left Abram, and pitched his tents close to the city of Sodom.

Abram lived instead in the land of Canaan.

'I have not forgotten my promise,' said God to Abram when Lot had gone. 'This land is yours. You will have so many descendants that no one will be able to count them. They will be as many as the grains of dust that fly in the wind. Now go, and explore the land that I have given you.'

Abram moved his tents near the great trees of Mamre at Hebron. He built an altar there and thanked God for all he had given him.

13 GOD'S PROMISE

Abram was living in the land God had given him. He had enough to eat and drink and took pleasure in his daily life, but there was something missing. God had promised him descendants. He and Sarai were no longer young and they still had no child.

'Don't be afraid, Abram,' said God. 'I will protect you. I will be everything you need.'

Abram trusted God. He told God about what he feared.

'Oh, Lord,' said Abram, 'how can you reward me and make my descendants great, when Sarai and I have no children? My servant, Eliezer, will inherit everything I have.'

'No,' said God. 'You will have a son who comes from your own body, a child who is yours in every way.' Then God said, 'Look up and count the stars! That's how many descendants you will have!'

Abram looked, and he believed what God had told him.

At sunset, Abram fell into a deep sleep. He dreamed, and God gave him a vision of what the future would hold.

'Your descendants will be strangers in a foreign land. They will live as slaves and be treated badly for 400 years. I will punish the nation who enslaves them and they will leave that country with great riches. Then they will return to this land, and it will all belong to them. And you, Abram, will live to a good old age, and die peacefully. This is my promise to you.'

14 SARAI'S MAIDSERVANT

Abram and Sarai lived for ten years in Canaan. Sarai knew what God had promised, but she had still had no children.

So Sarai decided to follow an ancient custom which would give Abram a child. She brought to Abram her Egyptian servant, Hagar.

'Take my servant, and let her be your wife too. Perhaps she will bear us a son.'

Abram did as Sarai asked, and took Hagar as his wife. Before long Hagar was pregnant. As soon as she knew that she was expecting Abram's child, she did not want Sarai to treat her as a servant any more. She began to despise Sarai because she could not have children.

'This is your fault!' Sarai complained unfairly to her husband. 'Hagar despises me.'

'Hagar is your servant,' replied Abram. 'Do what you think best.'

So Sarai started to ill-treat Hagar. Hagar became so unhappy that she ran away.

Hagar stopped by a spring in the desert and rested and drank some water there. Then an angel appeared and questioned her about where she had come from and where she was going.

'You must return to Sarai,' the angel commanded her, when she had admitted she had run away. 'God has seen how sad you are, but your

son will be special. You will call him Ishmael and he will have many descendants.'

Hagar was amazed.

'Now I know that God sees everything!' she said, and went back to Sarai. Some time later, Ishmael was born.

15 ABRAM WELCOMES STRANGERS

Ishmael grew up to be strong and made Abram happy. When Ishmael was 13 years old, God spoke again to Abram.

'I have not forgotten my promise,' God said. 'I will make you great. As a sign that you belong to me, all the men in your family and all your male servants must be circumcised. You will be called Abraham and Sarah, and by this time next year, Sarah will have a son called Isaac.'

Then Abraham and all the men among them were circumcised, just as God had said.

Some time later, when Abraham was resting outside his tent in the heat of the day, he noticed three strangers approaching. As was the custom, he went to make them welcome.

'Come and rest!' Abraham said to them. 'Let me bring you water to wash your feet, and something to eat.'

The men accepted Abraham's invitation, and he chose the best calf to be prepared and cooked for the visitors. They sat and ate while he stood apart under the trees.

'Where is your wife, Sarah?' they asked.

Immediately Abraham knew that he was in God's presence.

'She is there, inside the tent,' Abraham replied.

'By this time next year, Sarah will have a son.'

Sarah was listening at the entrance to the tent. She looked at her wrinkled skin and bent fingers, then laughed to herself.

'As if I could have a baby at my age!' she thought.

God knew what she was thinking.

'Is anything too hard for God?' said one of Abraham's visitors. 'You will have a son when I come again.'

16 ABRAHAM PRAYS FOR SODOM

The men prepared to leave Abraham and move on towards the cities of Sodom and Gomorrah.

'The people living in those cities do terrible things,' God told Abraham. 'I will visit them to see if what I hear is true. If it is, the city must be destroyed.'

Abraham looked down towards Sodom and thought about the people who lived in the city. His nephew, Lot, and his family still lived there.

'What if you find 50 good men?' Abraham asked God. 'Surely you won't destroy the city then.'

'No,' replied God. 'If I find 50 good men, it will be saved.'

'What if you find 45 good men?' asked Abraham.

'Then I won't destroy the city,' replied God.

'40?' Abraham pleaded.

'I won't destroy the city,' said God.

Abraham took a deep breath. 'Don't be angry with me,' he said. 'What if you find 30 good men?'

'I will spare the city,' promised God.

Once more Abraham spoke. '20?'

God promised to spare the people of Sodom.

'What if you find just ten good men?' asked Abraham.

'For the sake of ten good men, I will not destroy it,' said God finally.

17 RESCUE BY ANGELS

Lot was sitting in the gateway to the city of Sodom when the two men sent by God arrived. He offered them hospitality as Abraham had done earlier in the day.

'Thank you, but we will stay here,' they answered.

Lot was concerned for their safety.

'Please, you must come and stay in my house,' he insisted.

The angels agreed and Lot prepared them a meal in his home.

Outside the house, a crowd was gathering, blocking the way out. Fists thumped on the door. Loud voices demanded that Lot send the men out.

'We know you have two men staying with you,' they shouted. 'Hand them over!'

Lot went outside and tried to calm the crowd.

'These men are my guests,' he said. 'I cannot let you hurt them!'

'You're not one of us,' they shouted to Lot. 'It doesn't matter to us if you die first!'

The two angels pulled Lot inside the door, then struck the men outside with blindness so that Lot and his family could escape.

'Go quickly!' the angels said. 'Take your wife and daughters and leave now! This city will be destroyed by morning!'

The angels led them to the edge of the city.

'Run for your lives!' ordered the angels. 'Don't stop until you reach the mountains. And don't look back!'

The sun had risen by the time God sent down burning rain, destroying Sodom and Gomorrah. Lot's wife forgot the angels' warning. She looked back and was turned into a pillar of salt.

18 SARAH HAS A SON

'Who would believe that Abraham and I would have a son in our old age?' said Sarah, as she nursed Isaac.

God had fulfilled his promise. Sarah had become pregnant and given birth to a baby boy. She was happy at last.

As Isaac grew and became a little boy, Ishmael, Hagar's son, teased him. Sarah did not like it. Before long Sarah had convinced herself that Ishmael would steal her son's inheritance.

'I want you to make Hagar and her son leave,' she said to Abraham. 'It will not be good for Isaac if they stay here with us.'

But Ishmael was also Abraham's son. God spoke to Abraham.

'Do as Sarah asks, Abraham. I will take care of Hagar and her son. You will be blessed through Isaac.'

Abraham gave Hagar food and water and Hagar and Ishmael went into the desert.

When they ran out of water, Hagar thought they would die. She sat Ishmael in the shade of some bushes, and walked away so that she wouldn't see him suffer. God heard Ishmael weeping.

An angel spoke to Hagar. 'Don't be frightened,' he said. 'God knows your problems. Take Ishmael and carry on. I have promised that he will live to see his descendants.'

Then Hagar saw that there was a well from which she could draw water. She filled her water-skin and gave him a drink.

God looked after Ishmael as he grew up. He became a skilled archer and married an Egyptian woman.

19 GOD TESTS ABRAHAM

When Isaac was much older, Abraham heard God speak to him.

'Abraham!' God said one day. 'Take Isaac with you to a mountain in Moriah. I want you to give your precious son to me as a sacrifice.'

Abraham was stunned. His heart pounded. God had always been faithful to him. He had kept his promises. How could Abraham refuse to do this for God now?

Abraham cut wood for a fire and took Isaac and some servants with him on the three-day walk into the mountains. He made the last part of the journey with Isaac alone.

'Father,' asked Isaac, after they had walked a while in silence. 'We have brought wood for the sacrifice, but where is the lamb?'

'God will provide a lamb,' said Abraham sadly.

Abraham laid the wood on the stones for the altar. Then he tied his son's hands and placed him on the wood. Just as he lifted the knife to sacrifice the son he loved so much, he heard God's voice from heaven.

'Stop!' God said. 'You have shown me how much you love me. I will bless you, and you will have as many descendants as there are stars in the sky!'

Then Abraham saw a ram caught in a bush. God had provided the sacrifice. His son, Isaac, was safe.

20 WATER FOR TEN CAMELS

Sarah died, and Abraham grew older. He became anxious that his son should have a wife. He wanted to see his grandchildren before he died.

Abraham asked his servant to go on a journey to find a suitable young woman.

'Find a wife for Isaac,' said Abraham. 'I want him to marry a woman from our own people.'

So the servant took ten camels and expensive gifts and travelled back across the desert to the village where Abraham's brother lived.

The servant reached the well as the sun was setting. He made his camels kneel down as the women were coming from their homes to draw water. Then the servant prayed.

'Lord God of Abraham,' he prayed, 'be kind to us today so that we can find the wife you have chosen for Isaac. May she be the first girl who offers to draw water for me and all these camels.'

Before he had finished praying, Abraham's great-niece, Rebekah, came to draw water. Abraham's servant went to her and asked for a drink. Rebekah not only gave him water but she offered to water his ten camels. The servant watched as she went back to the well and filled her water jar again and again and again.

'She will be a kind wife for Isaac,' the servant thought.

21 A WIFE FOR ISAAC

Abraham's servant asked
Rebekah who she was and
whether he could stay with her
family that night.

When Rebekah told him, he was sure that God had led him there and
that this was his choice of a wife for Isaac.

Rebekah accepted the servant's gifts of a golden nose ring and two
bracelets and rushed home to tell her family about the man by the well.
Her brother Laban came to greet him and invited him back to their
home.

Servants came to feed the camels and a meal was prepared for him.
Abraham's servant would not eat until he had explained why he was
there. He told them about Abraham's wish to find a wife for Isaac from
his people. He told them about his prayer and the way that God had
answered that prayer by sending Rebekah.

Then the family were happy. They knew that this must be what God
wanted and would not prevent it happening. The servant brought to
them the gifts he had with him and they asked Rebekah if she was
happy to go back with the servant.

The next day they left together on the journey back to Abraham.

Isaac saw them as they drew near and went out to meet them. When
he heard the story, he was very happy. He married Rebekah and he
loved her.

22 ESAU AND JACOB

Isaac was 40 years old when he married Rebekah and he wanted very much to give grandchildren to his father, Abraham. Years went by and no children came.

Isaac prayed that God would bless them with a family just as his father had before him. God answered, and Rebekah found that she was expecting twins.

Two baby boys were born within minutes of each other. The first was covered in red hair; he was named Esau. The second was born holding on to his brother's heel; he was named Jacob.

The two boys were very different and soon it became clear that Esau was his father's favourite. Esau grew up to be a skilled hunter. Rebekah loved the younger brother best. He was a quiet young man and preferred to stay near their tents.

One day, Esau came home from hunting, hungry and tired. Jacob was cooking a spicy lentil stew.

'Hmmm… I would love some of that!' he said.

'Give me your birthright, and I will,' he said.

'I will die if I don't eat now!' said Esau. 'You're welcome to my inheritance!'

Then Esau ate the stew with some bread until he was full, and left Jacob. His birthright as the older son meant nothing to him.

23 ISAAC'S BLESSING

Isaac began to lose his sight as he grew older. He became frail and old and realised he might not have long to live. He called for his eldest son, Esau.

'Go and hunt some wild game and make my favourite meal for me,' he said. 'Then I will bless you.'

Esau took his bow and went out to hunt. It was years since he had given his birthright away and he had forgotten about it.

Rebekah had not forgotten.

'Go and kill two goats,' she ordered Jacob. 'I will cook for your father, and he will bless you instead of your brother.'

'Esau's skin is hairy,' he said. 'Father may not be able to see me, but I don't smell like Esau; and when he touches me, he will know I'm not my brother.'

Rebekah had already thought of that. She dressed Jacob in Esau's clothes and tied goatskin on to his arms and neck. She prepared the food and sent Jacob in to receive the blessing.

'Are you really Esau?' Isaac asked. 'Your voice does not sound right, yet you feel and smell like Esau.'

'I am,' Jacob lied. So Isaac blessed his younger son, Jacob, instead of Esau, his eldest.

When Esau found out he had been tricked, both he and his father were angry, but it was too late. The blessing had been given. Esau nursed a grudge against his brother, waiting until his father's death so that he could kill Jacob.

Rebekah did not intend to let this happen. She suggested to Isaac that Jacob go to her brother, Laban, to find a wife from among her own people, just as he had done when he married her.

Isaac sent Jacob to Laban, where Rebekah knew he would be safe.

24 JACOB'S DREAM

Jacob set out towards Haran, where his uncle Laban lived.

When it was night, Jacob lay down to sleep, with a stone as a pillow. He dreamed of a long flight of stairs, stretching from the earth at its foot into heaven itself. In his dream Jacob saw angels moving up and down the staircase. At the very top, Jacob saw God.

'I am the God of your father Isaac and your grandfather Abraham,' said God. 'I promise I will give to you and your descendants the land you are lying on. I will watch over you now and I will never leave you.'

When Jacob awoke, he knew that he had seen God and he was afraid. He took the stone he had used as a pillow and stood it up like a pillar to mark the special place where he had met with God.

'If you look after me as you have promised, I will obey you and follow you always,' said Jacob.

Then he continued his journey until he reached the place where his uncle lived with his family.

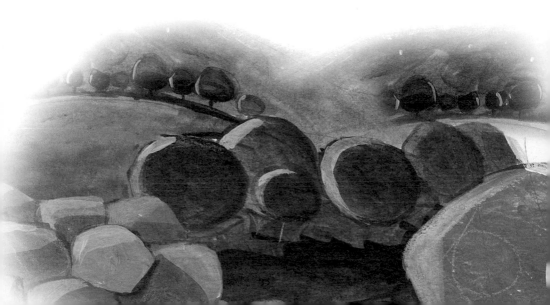

25 JACOB FALLS IN LOVE

Jacob asked some shepherds where they were from.

'We are from Haran,' they replied.

'Then you must know Laban?' he asked hopefully.

'Yes,' they replied. 'That's Laban's daughter, Rachel, over there.'

Jacob saw a beautiful girl leading her flock towards the well. He watered Rachel's sheep and told her he was her cousin. Soon Laban was welcoming him into his family.

After Jacob had stayed a month, Laban asked Jacob how he should be paid for working for his uncle.

Jacob thought carefully. He had fallen in love with Laban's youngest daughter, Rachel.

'I will work for you for seven years, if you let me marry Rachel,' said Jacob.

Laban agreed. Jacob worked hard, knowing that the time would come when he could have Rachel as his wife.

At the end of the seven years, Laban organised a big wedding feast. When the wedding took place, Rachel's older sister, Leah, was dressed in the bridal garments and covered with a veil. Instead of marrying Rachel, Jacob married Leah. When Jacob found out, it was too late.

'Why did you trick me?' asked Jacob angrily.

'It is our custom for the eldest to marry first,' replied Laban. 'I will let you marry Rachel now, if you agree to work for me for another seven years.'

Jacob agreed. He loved Rachel very much.

26 JACOB RUNS AWAY

God saw that Jacob did not love Leah and so he gave her children to love. She had six sons, Reuben, Simeon, Levi, Judah, Issachar and Zebulun, and a daughter named Dinah.

Rachel had no children, so she asked Jacob to take her maidservant as his wife. So Dan and Naphtali were born.

Jacob had a fourth wife when Leah gave Jacob her maidservant too. Gad and Asher were born.

Finally Rachel had a son of her own. She and Jacob were delighted. They called him Joseph and he became Jacob's favourite.

Jacob had now been with Laban for 20 years. God told Jacob it was time for him to return to his father's home.

'God has blessed me while you are here. Don't go,' said Laban.

'If I stay,' said Jacob, 'let me have any spotted or speckled sheep or goats from your herd. Then I can build up my own.'

Laban agreed, but secretly he took away every spotted or speckled animal so that Jacob would have to stay longer. Laban hadn't reckoned on God blessing all that Jacob did, however, so that soon Jacob owned many strong speckled and spotted animals.

Laban no longer felt happy to have Jacob as part of his family and Jacob felt unwelcome. The two men had started to trick each other. They could not trust each other. It was time to separate.

Secretly, Jacob prepared his wives and children for the long journey. He did not tell Laban they were going.

27 JACOB WRESTLES WITH GOD

Jacob left with Laban's daughters and his grandchildren, his healthy sheep and goats. He was now a man of great wealth. God had kept his promise to Jacob.

Jacob had left home in the first place because he had done a terrible thing to his twin brother. He knew it was time to return and say sorry.

Jacob sent his wives on ahead on camels. He was alone, sitting by the River Jabbok.

Then all at once a man appeared who started to wrestle with Jacob. They struggled all night long, each one trying to overpower the other. The man touched Jacob's hip and wrenched it so Jacob was in terrible pain, but still he would not give in.

Then the sky began to change colour as dawn broke.

'Let me go now,' said the man. 'The sun is rising.'

'No!' said Jacob. 'I will not let you go until you bless me.'

The man asked, 'What is your name?'

'Jacob!' came the reply.

'From now on you shall also be known as Israel,' said the man, 'for you have struggled with God and have not been defeated.'

Jacob limped away. He knew that this had been some sort of test. He had been wrestling with an angel sent by God. God had plans for him.

28 FRIENDS AND BROTHERS

Jacob was frightened. He had already sent messengers on ahead with gifts for his twin brother of sheep and goats, donkeys and camels.

Jacob had prayed to God. 'You told me to go back home,' said Jacob. 'You promised to protect me!'

Now Esau was coming to meet him, bringing 400 men with him. Jacob was certain that Esau wanted to kill him.

Jacob divided his family and herds into small groups. He hoped if Esau attacked one, the rest would escape.

Then Jacob went on ahead to meet his brother. Jacob bowed down to the ground. But Esau had not come to fight. He threw his arms around Jacob, and hugged him. Both men started to cry. Esau had forgiven Jacob. He was no longer angry. Neither was jealous of the other.

Jacob introduced Esau to his wives and children and they were friends and brothers once more.

Then Jacob made his way to Bethel where he settled with his family. He made an altar to thank God for keeping him safe and giving him so much. God gave Jacob the name Israel, and promised that his descendants, the Israelites, would number as many as the grains of sand in the desert.

29 RACHEL DIES

Jacob moved his tents towards Bethlehem. Rachel, the wife he loved the best, was expecting her second child any day.

While they were on the journey, Rachel began to give birth and she had another son. Rachel was weak and lived only long enough to know that her husband had named him Benjamin.

Rachel was buried near Bethlehem. Jacob then returned to the land of Mamre near Hebron where Abraham and Isaac had made their home.

Not long after, Isaac also died, having lived to a great age, and his twin sons buried him.

30 JACOB'S SPECIAL SON

Jacob now had twelve sons, but he loved Joseph more than his other children, and Joseph knew it.

By the time he was 17, Joseph helped his brothers to look after his father's flocks. Joseph watched them and listened to them, and then told his father the bad things they said and did.

Jacob gave Joseph a very special long-sleeved coat. When Joseph's brothers saw it, they knew that he was loved much more than they were. They hated him.

One night, Joseph dreamed. His dream was so strange that he told his brothers the next day.

'Listen to this!' he said. 'Last night I dreamed that we were all binding sheaves of corn when my sheaf stood up straight, and your sheaves bowed down before mine!'

This made his brothers even angrier than when their father had made him a beautiful coat!

'So do you plan to rule over us now?' they said.

Then Joseph dreamed again. This time he told his father too.

'I had another strange dream!' he said. 'I dreamed that the sun, the moon and eleven stars all bowed down before me!'

Jacob told Joseph not to boast in this way.

'Do you really think your mother and I as well as your brothers will bow down before you?' he asked.

His brothers hated Joseph even more. His father wondered what it all meant.

31 SOLD TO BE A SLAVE

Joseph's brothers had taken the sheep to graze. His father sent Joseph to find out how they were.

Joseph walked many miles across the desert until he found them not far from the ancient city of Dothan. His brothers saw him coming, dressed in the fine coat his father had given him.

'Here comes that dreamer,' they muttered to each other. By the time Joseph had come close to them, they had decided to kill him.

Reuben didn't like his younger brother, but he didn't want to be part of a plan to murder him.

'Let's not kill him,' Reuben said. 'Put him here in this empty well.'

As soon as Joseph reached them, the brothers tore off his coat and forced him down into the well. They were sitting eating a meal when they saw some Midianite traders, loaded up with spices, on their way to Egypt. It was not long before Judah had suggested a plan to sell their brother.

Joseph was pulled out of the well, sold for 20 pieces of silver and taken to Egypt to be sold as a slave. His brothers then slaughtered a goat and dipped Joseph's fine coat in the blood. They returned to their father and said they had found the coat.

Jacob believed that his much-loved son had been attacked by a wild animal and was dead. He was overcome with grief.

32 PRISON DREAMS

Joseph was taken to Egypt and sold to Potiphar, the captain of the guard.

Joseph worked hard and God blessed Potiphar's home because of him. Soon Potiphar trusted him with everything he owned and Joseph became his chief servant.

Joseph had grown into a strong, good-looking young man. Potiphar's wife saw this and wanted him for herself. Joseph was a good servant and kept away from her. This made her so angry that she claimed that he had attacked her. Potiphar believed his wife and had Joseph thrown into prison.

Once more Joseph worked hard, even though things were difficult for him. God did not abandon him. He blessed Joseph again so that soon he was put in charge of the other prisoners.

After a while, Joseph was put in charge of Pharaoh's personal servant and cook, who were also in prison. When they each had a strange dream, Joseph told them that God could help them to understand the meanings of the dreams. This meant bad news for the cook. He was executed by Pharaoh soon afterwards. There was good news for the personal servant, who was released, as Joseph predicted.

The personal servant did not speak up for Joseph when he was free again. He forgot all about him.

33 PHARAOH'S STRANGE DREAMS

Two long years went by. Joseph remained in prison.

Then Pharaoh had strange and disturbing dreams. No one could explain them to him, but he believed they must mean something important. The personal servant then remembered Joseph.

'There is a man in your prison who can help,' he said, and he told Pharaoh what had happened when he and the cook had also had strange dreams.

Pharaoh sent for Joseph and told him what he had dreamed.

'In the first dream, seven thin cows ate up seven fat, healthy cows,' said Pharaoh. 'In the second dream, seven thin, straggly ears of corn ate up seven healthy ears of corn.'

'Both dreams have the same meaning,' said Joseph. 'God is warning you that there will be seven years of good harvest followed by seven years of famine. If you store the grain wisely, you and your people will survive.'

Pharaoh knew immediately who should help him look after all the grain: he put Joseph in charge of the whole land of Egypt. He put a ring on Joseph's finger and a gold chain around his neck. Pharaoh had him ride in a chariot dressed in fine robes, and wherever Joseph went, people bowed down to him.

Joseph was 30 years old when his dreams began to come true.

34 FAMINE IN CANAAN

Over the next seven years there were abundant harvests. Joseph made sure that all the extra grain was stored carefully. Then, as the harvests failed in Egypt and in all the lands around them, Joseph opened the storehouses and sold the grain to the Egyptians. Everyone had what they needed to get through the seven years of famine.

Back in Canaan, Jacob heard that there was grain in Egypt. He sent ten of his sons to buy some. Jacob kept only his youngest son, Benjamin, at home with him.

When the brothers arrived, they went to the Egyptian governor and bowed down before him. Many years had passed since they had sold their brother into slavery. They did not expect to see him there; they did not expect to see him dressed as a ruler with power to save their lives. None of the brothers recognised Joseph in the man before them.

Joseph, however, knew that the men on their knees were his father's sons. He did not speak to them in the language of the Israelites, but used an interpreter, so they would not know he understood them.

'Are you spies?' Joseph asked them.

'No, sir,' they replied. 'We are brothers from Canaan. Our youngest brother is at home with our father. We are hungry and have come to buy food.'

'I don't believe you!' Joseph said. 'You must prove this by bringing your brother here to me.'

Then Joseph had them put in prison to think about what he had said.

35 SIMEON IS TAKEN HOSTAGE

After three days, Joseph released his brothers from prison. 'Go home,' he said, 'but as proof you are not spies, leave someone here and return to me with your father's youngest son.'

'This is all our own fault!' the brothers said in their own language. 'Joseph pleaded with us for his life but we wouldn't listen. We did a terrible wrong and now we are being punished!'

Joseph understood all they said. He wept for the wasted years.

Then Joseph had Simeon taken from them and bound up. He sold grain to his brothers and sent them home, but secretly had all their silver replaced in their sacks.

That night, the brothers opened their grain sacks to feed their donkeys, and found that the money they had paid for the grain had been returned. What could have happened?

When the brothers returned to Jacob, they told him everything. They explained they must return with Benjamin or Simeon would die.

Jacob shook his head.

'Once I had twelve sons,' he said. 'Joseph was lost many years ago; now I have lost Simeon. Benjamin is the only son left to me from his mother, Rachel. I cannot let him go. If anything happens to him, I will surely die of sorrow.'

So Benjamin did not go. The family lived through the famine by eating the grain they had brought back from Egypt until there was no more left.

36 JACOB LETS BENJAMIN GO

'You must go back to Egypt for more grain,' Jacob said to his sons, 'or we will all die of hunger!'

Judah would not return without Benjamin.

'We were warned what would happen,' he told his father. 'You will lose all your sons if you will not take this risk. Either we go with Benjamin or we die here of starvation.'

So Jacob made sure that his sons packed not only silver to pay for more grain, but also enough to replace the silver they had brought back from Egypt. Then he packed honey and spices, pistachio nuts and almonds, as gifts for the Egyptian governor.

Then, very sadly, Jacob let his youngest son go with them to Egypt.

37 JOSEPH'S FEAST

When the brothers arrived, they went to the governor with Benjamin. They quickly explained to Joseph's steward that they had found their silver in their grain sacks and had brought it back.

'Don't be afraid,' the man told them. 'Your God is taking care of you. I was paid for the grain you bought. God made sure that you had silver to return to your country.'

Then Simeon was returned to them safely and all the brothers were invited to a feast at Joseph's house. They gave him their gifts, but they still did not realise that the great man in front of them was their lost brother, Joseph.

Joseph asked after their father, and then, when he saw his younger brother, Benjamin, he wept privately for joy. When the brothers sat down to the feast, Joseph made sure that Benjamin had more to eat and drink than anyone else. The brothers could not understand their good fortune.

38 THE SILVER CUP

When the time came for the men to return to their father, Joseph arranged for them to be given as much grain as they could carry. As before, he made sure that their silver was also put back in their sacks. Finally, he asked his servant to put his own silver cup in Benjamin's sack. As the brothers left the city, Joseph told his men to catch up with them and accuse them of stealing the silver cup.

The brothers were shocked. They denied that any one of them could be guilty of stealing from the man who had treated them so well. They were so sure that they said that if anyone was found to have stolen the cup, that brother would die, and all the others would become slaves in Egypt…

Their bags were searched, beginning with the oldest brother. When the silver cup was found in Benjamin's sack, the brothers tore their clothes in disbelief.

'Please don't harm Benjamin!' Judah pleaded. 'We will all become your slaves rather than that!'

'There is no need,' Joseph said. 'You may all go back to your father. I will make only Benjamin my slave.'

Then Judah asked to speak to Joseph alone. He explained that his father would die of grief if anything happened to Benjamin. He begged to be allowed to take his place for  the sake of his aged father.

39 JACOB'S LOST SON

Joseph ordered his servants to leave him alone with his brothers. Then he wept so loudly that all his household heard him.

'I am your brother, Joseph,' he told them. 'You sold me into slavery, and you wished me harm, but God meant only that good should come of it. There will be famine for another five years yet. God made sure I was here in Egypt and helped me to become known to Pharaoh so that your lives could be saved.

'Now you must return to our father. Tell him that I am governor of all Egypt and that it is safe for him to come here. You will live in the land of Goshen with your families and sheep and goats and all that you own; and you will have plenty to eat during the famine.'

Joseph's brothers wept for joy. God had blessed them in ways they could not have imagined.

When Jacob heard all that had happened, he could hardly believe it. His son Joseph was still alive! He agreed to leave the land of Canaan and took all his children and grandchildren with him to live in Egypt.

40 JACOB DIES IN EGYPT

Joseph went in his chariot to meet his father in the land of Goshen. There was much weeping as the two men threw their arms around each other.

Jacob and his family then settled in Goshen and made it their home. God blessed them and soon they had property there, and many grandchildren and great-grandchildren were born to Jacob. He lived in Egypt for 17 years, and when he knew it was time for him to die, he made Joseph promise that he would be buried in the land of his ancestors, not in Egypt.

Joseph had married and had two sons of his own: Manasseh and Ephraim. Joseph brought the boys to see his father as he lay dying.

'I never thought I would see you again, my son,' he said to Joseph. 'Now I am able to see not just you, but also your sons. God will be with you all. He will take you back to the land he promised to give to my grandfather, Abraham, to my father, Isaac, and to me, and he will bless you.'

Jacob blessed each one of his sons, and then he died. Joseph wept over his father and then he had him embalmed in the way of the Egyptians. He asked permission from Pharaoh, and then he took his father's body back to Canaan to bury him.

41 SLAVES IN EGYPT

Joseph lived to see his own great-great-grandchildren. Before his death, he told his brothers that God would one day take them back to the promised land. Then Joseph died and was embalmed, and was buried in a coffin in Egypt.

Years passed, and Joseph's descendants began to number hundreds of thousands of people. A time came when the new Pharaoh looked at the Israelites who lived in Egypt, and he was afraid.

'There are too many of them,' he said. 'Soon they will join with our enemies and overcome us. We must enslave them and make them build us new cities.'

So the Egyptians oppressed the Israelites. They made them work hard for them and ill-treated them. Still the Israelites seemed to grow in number and God blessed them.

Then Pharaoh ordered the midwives to kill all baby boys born to the Israelite women. The midwives would not obey Pharaoh; they told him that the women were strong and gave birth before they arrived to help. God blessed the Egyptian midwives. But Pharaoh had another plan. He gave an order that all baby boys must be thrown into the River Nile and drowned.

42 MIRIAM AND THE PRINCESS

One day an Israelite woman gave birth to a son. She hid him until he was three months old. She could not let the Egyptians take her baby away.

Then when he was too big to hide any longer, she put the baby in a basket. She coated it with tar to make it waterproof, and told her daughter, Miriam, to hide it in the reeds along the bank of the River Nile.

When the Pharaoh's daughter came to bathe in the river, she heard the sound of a baby crying and felt sorry for him.

'Shall I find someone to nurse him for you?' asked Miriam, who was watching nearby.

'Yes,' said the princess. 'I will keep this baby and call him Moses.'

Miriam went to fetch her mother.

'Look after this baby until he is old enough to live with me,' said the princess. Miriam's mother took her little son away to care for him.

43 MOSES KILLS A SLAVEDRIVER

Moses grew up strong and healthy. He lived with the Egyptians, but he saw how badly his own people were treated.

One day, Moses stood and watched the Israelites working under the hot sun. He saw the marks on their bodies where they had been beaten. He saw the sweat dripping from their brows. Then he saw an Egyptian beating one of Moses' own people.

Moses had seen enough.

Looking around to make sure no one was watching him, Moses seized the Egyptian and killed him. Then he buried the man's body in the sand.

The next day, Moses saw two Israelites fighting.

'Why are you hurting each other?' he asked them.

'What does it matter to you?' one of the men replied. 'Are you going to kill me as you killed that Egyptian?'

Moses was frightened. He realised someone had seen the killing. Soon the news would reach Pharaoh… Moses prepared to leave before Pharaoh issued orders for his death. He ran away to Midian.

44 THE ANGEL IN THE BURNING BUSH

Moses made his home in Midian. He married Zipporah, one of seven daughters born to Jethro, the priest, and had a son called Gershom.

Moses was in the desert in Horeb, looking after his father-in-law's sheep one day, when he saw something strange. A bush was on fire but the flames did not burn it up. Moses went over to take a closer look.

'Moses! Moses!' called a voice from the flames.

'Yes, here I am,' he replied.

'Take off your shoes!' ordered the angel of the Lord from the burning bush. 'You are on holy ground.'

Moses was so afraid, he hid his face.

'I am the God of Abraham, the God of Isaac and the God of Jacob. I have seen how my people, the Israelites, are suffering as slaves in Egypt. I want them to be free to live in the land I have promised them. I want you to go to Pharaoh and bring my people out of Egypt.'

Moses was amazed.

'I can't go to Pharaoh,' said Moses. 'Why would he listen to me?'

'I will help you,' replied God.

45 MOSES IS AFRAID

Moses was afraid. He did not want to be the Israelites' leader.

'What shall I say?' said Moses.

'Tell them that the God of Abraham, the God of Isaac and the God of Jacob sent you to bring them out of slavery in Egypt. Now throw your staff on the ground,' ordered God.

Moses threw it. The staff hit the ground and turned into a snake. Moses ran from the snake.

'Now pick it up by its tail,' said God.

As Moses picked it up, it changed back into a staff.

'Put your hand inside your cloak,' said God.

When Moses took his hand out from under his cloak, it was white with leprosy. Quickly, he put it back and when he removed it, his hand was whole and healthy again.

'Show them these things,' said God, 'and they will know that I have sent you.'

'I do not speak well,' said Moses finally. 'I have always found it difficult to speak to people. Please send someone else.'

'I made you, and I know all about you,' God said. 'I can help you. Your brother Aaron can go with you. He will speak for you.'

Then Moses started making arrangements to return to Egypt.

46 BRICKS WITHOUT STRAW

God sent Aaron to meet Moses and he explained all that God had told him to do. Then they went to the people and told them that God had heard their cries for help. They performed the signs that God had given to Moses and the people believed that God had sent him to help them.

Then, together, Moses and Aaron went to see Pharaoh.

'We have come with a message from the Lord, the God of Israel: "Let my people go, so that they can worship me," ' they said.

'I don't know your God,' said Pharaoh, 'and I don't want to let the Israelites go. They are my slaves, and I need them to work.'

Then Pharaoh gave new orders to his slavedrivers.

'Let the Israelites gather their own straw to make bricks. They must work even harder to produce just as many bricks as before!'

'How can we make the same number of bricks without straw?'

'You are lazy,' said Pharaoh. 'Get back to work!'

Some of the Israelites went and complained to Moses.

'This is your fault!' they said. 'Pharaoh hates us even more!'

Then Moses spoke to God.

'Why have you allowed me to cause such trouble?' he asked.

'They are my people,' promised God. 'I will rescue them.'

47 PLAGUES IN EGYPT

Moses and Aaron went to see Pharaoh again.

'The Lord, the God of Israel says: "Let my people go, so that they can worship me,"' they said.

Just as before, Pharaoh refused to let the Israelites go.

God spoke to Moses.

'Tell Aaron to stretch out his staff,' he said.

Aaron stretched out his staff, and the water in Egypt turned to blood. All the fish in the Nile died; the smell was terrible throughout the land.

Moses and Aaron went to see Pharaoh again.

'The Lord, the God of Israel says: "Let my people go, so that they can worship me,"' they said. 'If you refuse, God will send a plague of frogs.'

Just as before, Pharaoh refused to let the Israelites go.

Aaron stretched out his staff, and Egypt was covered in frogs. Then Pharaoh agreed to let the people go, as long as God took away the frogs.

Moses asked God and the frogs all died. Then Pharaoh changed his mind. He refused to let the Israelites go.

Seven more times Moses and Aaron asked Pharaoh to let the Israelites go. When Pharaoh refused, God sent plagues of gnats and flies; every Egyptian animal died, and the people were covered in boils; violent hailstorms battered the land and then it was covered in locusts, and finally, the whole of Egypt was plunged into darkness.

After each plague, Pharaoh agreed to let the Israelites go, but as soon as God took away the plague, Pharaoh changed his mind.

48 THE FINAL PLAGUE

'I will give Pharaoh one more warning,' said God to Moses. 'If he still refuses to listen, every Egyptian, including Pharaoh, will want you to leave.'

Then God told Moses that this time the firstborn of every living creature in Egypt would die including Pharaoh's own son. God would protect his people and keep them safe. He gave Moses special instructions to follow.

Moses warned Pharaoh, but Pharaoh would not listen. He did not want the Israelites to leave Egypt.

That night every Israelite family coated their door frames with blood from a lamb, so that the angel of death would pass over them. They ate a special meal of roast lamb with unleavened bread and herbs with their cloaks wrapped round them, their sandals on their feet, and a staff in their hands.

'This night must never be forgotten,' Moses told the people. 'We must tell our children and our grandchildren everything that happens tonight.'

That night, after midnight, every firstborn Egyptian died. The cries of the Egyptians could be heard throughout the land.

49 PHARAOH LETS THE PEOPLE GO

Pharaoh called Moses and Aaron and told them to go.

'Take your cattle and sheep and leave this land!' he shouted.

The Egyptians gave the Israelites gold and silver—sall they asked for.

Then Moses told the people that God would lead them to Canaan.

By day God appeared to the people as a pillar of cloud leading them, and by night God was a pillar of fire. God did not take them by the road that crossed the land of the Philistines but by the desert road towards the Red Sea.

50 CROSSING THE RED SEA

It was not long before Pharaoh began to regret that he had let his slaves leave Egypt. He decided to bring them back.

Pharaoh took 600 of his best chariots and every other chariot he could find in Egypt; he took horses, horsemen and troops on foot. The Israelites soon saw that they were coming after them and were terrified.

'Were there no graves in Egypt?' they demanded of Moses. 'Have you brought us here into the desert to die?'

Moses was not afraid. He knew that God would save his people.

The pillar of cloud moved behind the people so it stood between them and the Egyptians and brought confusion to Pharaoh's men.

Then Moses stretched out his hand over the Red Sea and God sent a wind to blow back the waters through the night so that all the Israelites could pass over safely to the other side on dry land.

The Egyptians started to follow, but Moses stretched out his hand again, now from the safety of the far bank, and God sent back the water to cover Pharaoh's army in the Red Sea. None of the Egyptians survived, but all God's people were safe.

51 GOD IS GREAT

When Moses and the Israelites saw what had happened to the
Egyptians, they wanted to tell God how great and wonderful he was: he
had saved them from years of suffering. So Moses led the Israelites in a
song of praise.

'Our God is great and mighty!

He threw horses and riders into the sea.

Our God is strong and mighty!

He came to rescue us all.

He came for us as he promised,

He loves us and leads us.'

Then Miriam, Moses' sister, took her tambourine, and began to play
and to dance. She wanted to thank God for all that he had
done. The other Israelite women saw what she did, and they
followed her, dancing and playing tambourines.

'Sing to the Lord God,' sang Miriam. 'He is the greatest!'

52 WANDERING IN THE DESERT

Moses led the Israelites into the desert beyond the sea. They walked in the heat of the sun for three days but found no water. When they found it, it tasted bitter and they could not drink it.

The people grumbled and complained. Moses spoke to God.

'Throw that piece of wood into the water,' said God.

Moses obeyed God, and the water became sweet to drink.

The people rested and then travelled on through the desert. Soon they were grumbling again.

'If only we had died in our beds in Egypt!' the people said to Moses. 'At least we didn't go hungry there.'

God heard the grumblings of his people.

'In the mornings I will make bread fall from the sky like rain. In the evenings I will provide quail for you to eat. Collect just enough for your daily needs, and on the day before the sabbath day, collect twice as much so the sabbath can be a day of rest.'

Everything happened just as God had said. They called the bread that God gave them 'manna'. It looked like a thin layer of frost on the ground and it tasted like wafers made from honey. God continued to provide bread for the people every day that they wandered in the desert.

53 WATER FROM THE ROCK

The Israelites continued to wander through the desert, moving camp as God led them on.

Soon they were grumbling again. They could find no water to drink.

'We must have water!' they complained to Moses.

So Moses called to God to help him. He was sure the people were angry enough to kill him if he couldn't find water for them.

God answered Moses. He told Moses to take with him some of the people and go to the rock at Horeb where he should hit it with his staff. If he did this, said God, water would pour from the rock and the people would have good water to drink.

Moses did as God instructed and water poured from the rock in front of the people, just as God had said.

54 THE BATTLE WITH THE AMALEKITES

When the Israelites reached Rephidim, they were attacked by the Amalekites, the tribal people who lived in that part of the desert. It was clear that they wanted to fight; Moses had no choice but to defend the Israelites.

Moses told Joshua to choose men to make up an army.

The next day, Moses, his brother Aaron and Hur went up the hill overlooking the desert valley where the battle would take place. Moses held out his staff over the fighting men and watched the battle. For as long as he held up his staff, Joshua's men were the stronger side; when Moses tired and lowered his staff, the Amalekites seemed to take control of the battle.

So Hur and Aaron found a large stone for Moses to sit on. Then they stood on either side of him and supported his arms so Moses could hold up the staff until sunset, when the Amalekites were defeated.

Then Moses made an altar to thank God for protecting them against the enemy. He called it 'The Lord is my banner' because he had lifted his staff high in the air.

55 GOD SPEAKS FROM THE MOUNTAIN

After three months in the desert, the Israelites camped at the foot of Mount Sinai.

Moses climbed the mountain and God told him what he was to tell the people.

'You have seen how I saved you from the Egyptians and brought you safely across the Red Sea. Now I will make a promise to you: you will be my special people if you will obey me, and keep your side of the agreement.'

Moses told the people what God had said and they promised to obey.

God told Moses that he would come down and speak to him on the mountain when they heard the sound of a ram's horn. The people were to prepare themselves and keep their distance until then.

Three days later, thunder and lightning struck, and there was a thick cloud over the mountain. At the sound of a trumpet blast, Moses led the people to the foot of the mountain. There was fire and smoke, the ground shook, and the trumpet sounded over and over again so that the Israelites trembled.

Then God came to the mountaintop, and Moses went up to meet him.

56 THE TEN COMMANDMENTS

God gave Moses the laws for his people to obey. He engraved them on two stone tablets, in his own hand.

'I am the Lord your God, who brought you out of Egypt where you were slaves. Do not worship any god but me.

'Do not make idols that look like anything in the sky or on the earth or in the ocean under the earth. Don't bow down and worship idols.

'Do not misuse my name. I am the Lord your God.

'Remember that the sabbath day belongs to me. You have six days when you can do your work, but the seventh day of each week belongs to me, your God. No one is to work on that day.

'Respect your father and your mother, and you will live a long time in the land I am giving you.

'Do not murder.

'Be faithful to your marriage partner.

'Do not steal.

'Do not tell lies about others.

'Do not want anything that belongs to someone else. Don't want anyone's house, wife or husband, slaves, oxen, donkeys or anything else.'

57 A SPECIAL PLACE FOR GOD

God not only gave Moses commandments so the people would know how best to live lives that pleased him, but he also told him how he wanted the people to worship him.

God told Moses that they were to build a special tent, a tabernacle. It should have linen curtains made from blue, purple and scarlet-coloured yarn. The altar should be made of acacia wood and all the bowls and shovels and meat forks should be made of bronze.

There should be a golden lampstand with six branches, the cup of each one shaped like almond flowers. The table should be decorated with gold.

God also gave instructions about what the priests should wear. As well as the fine linen garments, they should wear a breastplate decorated with twelve beautiful stones—ruby, topaz, beryl, turquoise, sapphire, emerald, jacinth, agate, amethyst, chrysolite, onyx and jasper—each one to represent one of the twelve tribes of Israel.

'I have chosen Bezalel and Oholiab to do the work,' God said to Moses. 'I have filled Bezalel with my Spirit so that he will be able to work with many different materials. I will help all the craftsmen to use their gifts.'

When God had finished talking to Moses, he gave him the two stone tablets and Moses took them down the mountain.

58 THE GOLDEN CALF

Moses stayed on the mountain talking with God for 40 days and 40 nights.

At first the people waited, wondering what news Moses would bring from God. Day by day passed. The longer the people waited, the more tired and restless they became.

'Where has Moses gone?' they asked Aaron eventually. 'Anything could have happened to him in all this time. We cannot wait any longer. Make us gods that we can see and touch!'

Aaron knew immediately what to do. The Egyptians had worshipped many golden statues while they had been Pharaoh's slaves. Aaron told the people to give him all their gold jewellery. Then he melted it down, and made it into the shape of one of the Egyptian gods. It was a golden calf.

The people were delighted. They thanked the golden calf for leading them out of Egypt. Aaron realised that this was against God's law. He built an altar and announced that the following day would be a festival to the Lord.

Meanwhile God had seen the making of the golden calf.

'Go back to the people,' God told Moses. 'Already they have forgotten that I have brought them out of Egypt. They have made an idol to worship.'

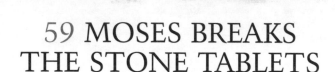

59 MOSES BREAKS THE STONE TABLETS

Moses hurried down the mountain, carrying the two stone tablets on which God's ten commandments were written. Joshua was waiting for him. Together they heard the noise the people were making.

'The people are shouting! Perhaps they are being attacked?'

'This is not the sound of battle!' Moses replied. 'This is the sound of singing and dancing. The people are having a party.'

Moses went closer and saw the way the people were dancing around the golden calf. God's laws were broken. Moses threw the stone tablets down at the bottom of the mountain. Now they were also broken.

Then Moses destroyed the golden calf.

'How could you let this happen?' he asked Aaron angrily.

'The people wanted this,' muttered Aaron. 'I gave them what they asked for.'

'God will punish those who have broken his commandments!' said Moses. Then he turned to the people.

'Who is on the Lord's side?' he asked them. 'Anyone who still loves God, come here to me.'

Many of the people came to Moses; many more did not.

'God will bless those people who stand firm and worship only him. He will punish those who do not. I will speak to God and ask for his mercy.'

A plague swept through the people and many died because the people had worshipped the golden calf.

60 MOSES ASKS FOR GOD'S MERCY

God was very angry with the Israelites.

'I made a promise to Abraham, Isaac and to Jacob which I cannot break,' said God. 'I promised that their descendants would live in a land that I would give them. Leave this place, take the people, and go to the promised land. Because they have disobeyed me, I will not go with you.'

When the people heard what God had said, they were sorry. They wanted God to stay with them.

Moses used to pitch a special tent away from the main camp. Joshua would stand outside. When Moses needed to ask God something, he would go inside and a pillar of cloud would cover the entrance. Then God would speak to Moses as if they were friends. The Israelites would stand by their own tents and watch. They would worship God until Moses returned to the camp.

Now Moses spoke to God on behalf of all the people.

'If you are pleased with me, Lord, and will hear me, please teach me your ways. Help me to serve you better. You have called us your own people. If you will not go with us, how are we different from any other group of people? We need you. Please don't send us on alone to the promised land.'

61 THE CLEFT IN THE ROCK

God saw that Moses wanted to obey him and save his people.

'I will do what you ask,' he said. 'I love my people. I love you and I know you.'

'Let me know you better,' asked Moses. 'Let me see your glory.'

'No one can see my face and live,' said God. 'There is a place where you can stand on the mountain and I will pass by you. You must stand in the cleft of the rock and I will cover you with my hand to protect you, but you cannot see my face.'

God told Moses to come alone to the mountain the following morning with two new stone tablets.

Moses stood in the cleft of the rock on Mount Sinai. God came and passed in front of him as he had promised. Then God spoke.

'I am the Lord. I am faithful and compassionate. I love the people I have made and I long to forgive their disobedience.'

Moses fell on the ground and worshipped God.

'I will make a covenant with you, a special promise,' said God. 'I will lead you to the land I promised to give Abraham and his descendants. But if you disobey my laws, I will punish you.'

God wrote the commandments on the new stone tablets and gave Moses other laws to help the people obey him.

When the people saw Moses, they were afraid to go near him—his face shone because he had been in God's presence.

62 THE CLOUD OF GOD'S PRESENCE

Moses told the people about the special tent they needed to make for God.

'We need to make an ark, a table, an altar and a lampstand, and there will be special clothes for the priests to wear. If you are willing, give God anything you have that can be used.'

The people brought their gold, silver, bronze and precious jewels. The women spun linen and made cloth out of goat's hair. They brought the best spices and the purest olive oil. They worked for six days of the week, and rested on the seventh, as God had commanded.

When the people had finished making everything for the tent of meeting, Moses was pleased with them. The stone tablets were placed inside the ark and this was put in the 'Holy of Holies', separated by a curtain.

Aaron and his sons prepared to be God's priests. They washed themselves and dressed in the special clothes God had designed for them.

Moses set a courtyard around the tent of meeting, made with more curtains. Then a cloud covered the tent, and God's presence filled it. His presence was so great that Moses could not enter.

God's presence remained with the Israelites, just as he had promised. When the cloud lifted, it was time to move on, with God leading the way.

63 MIRIAM AND AARON GRUMBLE

For some time the Israelites travelled through the desert. Whenever the cloud rested, they made camp. When the cloud lifted, they moved on towards the land God had promised them.

Soon they found their journey hard. They started to complain about their hardships and they complained about the food. They began to wish they were back in Egypt where they had meat whenever they wanted it and sweet melons and cucumbers. They blamed Moses for everything.

Even Miriam and Aaron complained. They gossiped about Moses' wife and spoke against their brother.

'Why is Moses so special?' they asked. 'Can God not also speak through us?'

God heard what they said.

'Listen carefully to what I have to say,' said God. 'I have spoken to Moses face to face and he is faithful to me. Who are you to challenge him?'

When the cloud of God's presence lifted, Miriam saw that her skin was covered in leprosy.

'Forgive us, Lord!' cried Aaron to Moses. 'Please don't let Miriam suffer like this!'

Moses also cried out to God for Miriam to be healed.

'She must stay outside the camp for seven days,' said God. 'Then she can return.'

The people waited. They did not continue their journey until Miriam had returned to the camp.

64 SPIES IN THE LAND

As the Israelites approached Canaan, God told Moses to send one man from each of the twelve tribes to explore the promised land.

Moses sent them to find out who lived there, how the cities were fortified and how fertile the land was. When the men returned, two of them were carrying a heavy branch bearing a single cluster of juicy grapes. They also brought figs and pomegranates.

Moses gathered everyone to listen to the spies' report.

'The land is good and fertile,' said the spies. 'It would be a wonderful place to live. Just look at this fruit!'

But it was not all good news.

'We saw strong, powerful people as big as giants, living in walled cities,' warned ten of the spies. 'They are too strong for us to fight.'

Then the Israelites were miserable. They cried. They grumbled.

'Let's choose another leader,' they said, 'and go back to Egypt.'

Moses and Aaron got down on their knees in front of all the Israelites. Joshua and Caleb, the other two spies, joined them.

'God has promised to give us this wonderful land. Trust him.'

The Israelites would not believe them. They planned to stone them to death. Then God appeared at the tent of meeting.

'Will you not trust me?' asked God. 'Those who have doubted will wander in the desert for 40 years. Only their children will enter Canaan. But Caleb and Joshua will live in the promised land.'

65 40 YEARS IN THE DESERT

When the Israelites heard what God had said, they were sorry.

'We will do what God wanted,' they said. 'We will go and fight the people who live in the land so that we can make our home in Canaan.'

'It's too late now!' cried Moses. 'You cannot enter the land safely without God's help. He made a promise and you refused to believe him. If you go into the land, you will be defeated. God will not go with you.'

Moses would not move from the camp. He stayed with the ark of God's covenant.

The Israelites did not listen to him. They went into the hill country where they were attacked by both the Canaanites and the Amalekites, and were defeated.

Then the Israelites moved back from the borders of Canaan, and made their way towards the desert. For 40 years they wandered there, eating the manna that God provided for their daily needs.

66 MOSES STRIKES THE ROCK

Life in the desert was hard. By the time the Israelites had been there for 40 years, many of those who had lived in Egypt had died. Their descendants arrived at Kadesh and there, Miriam died and was buried. The people were faced with no water again. A new generation of Israelites began to doubt God's care for them.

'Why did you bring us here?' they moaned to Moses and Aaron. 'This is a terrible place. We are thirsty, and there is no water here.'

Aaron and Moses left the people and went to the tent of meeting.

'Take your staff,' said God to Moses, 'and gather the people so that they can see what I can do. This time just speak to the rock, and it will pour out water.'

Moses took his staff and gathered the people to watch him. He was angry. He had heard their fathers moaning and their descendants were no better. Instead of obeying God, he held his staff in the air, and then hit the rock with it twice.

Immediately, water poured out from the rock and the people had plenty for their needs.

God was not pleased with Moses and Aaron.

'You did not do what I said,' said God.

67 THE DEATH OF AARON

As the Israelites approached the land of Edom, they sent messengers to ask if they could go through their country.

'You cannot pass this way,' warned the Edomites. 'We will come with swords if you try!'

The Israelites asked again, but the Edomites came with a large army and turned God's people back from their borders.

So the people came instead to Mount Hor. Here God told Moses to call Aaron to go to the top of the mountain with his son Eleazar.

'It is time for Aaron to pass on his priestly duties to his son before he dies,' said God. So Moses took Aaron's special clothes and dressed his son in them.

Soon afterwards, Aaron died. He was mourned by all the Israelites for 30 days.

68 THE SNAKE ON A POLE

Again the people travelled around Edom to go to the Red Sea because they could not go through the Edomites' land.

They began to grumble once more. First it was the lack of water; then they grumbled to one another about the bread that God provided for them. God heard their grumblings and sent poisonous snakes to slither through the camp and bite them.

The Israelites realised that God was angry with them.

'We have sinned,' they cried to Moses. 'We shouldn't have complained. God has saved us from our enemies. Ask God to take the snakes away.'

So Moses prayed.

'Make a bronze snake and put it on a pole,' said God. 'Anyone who has been bitten should look at the snake on the pole and they will be healed; they will not die.'

Moses did as God told him. Those who looked at the snake lived.

69 TWO VICTORIES IN BATTLE

When the Israelites came to Moab, they asked Sihon, king of the Amorites, if they could pass through peacefully. Sihon had already fought for the land and taken it from the Moabites. Sihon would not let them pass through.

Sihon brought his whole army together and marched into the desert to defend his land. The Israelites fought back. They began to take Sihon's land. When they had defeated Sihon, the Israelites settled there.

Moses then led the people towards Bashan. King Og marched towards them. He did not want the Israelites in his land.

'Don't be afraid,' God told Moses. 'This victory will also be yours.'

So Moses and the people fought King Og until he and his army were also defeated.

Then the Israelites took the land and camped along the Jordan in the plains of Moab. The walls of the city of Jericho were on the other side of the river.

70 BALAAM'S DONKEY

Balak, king of Moab, saw what had happened to King Sihon and to King Og. He saw the large number of Israelites and he was frightened for his own land and people.

'Tell Balaam, the sorcerer, to curse the Israelites so that I can defeat them,' he ordered. 'Give him as much money as he wants.'

God warned Balaam not to listen to Balak's messengers.

Balaam heard God's warning, but decided to go to Balak anyway. He saddled his donkey, and set off next morning.

God was angry with Balaam. He sent an angel with a drawn sword to stand in his path. Balaam did not see the angel, but his donkey did. She veered off the road, and into the field. Balaam beat the donkey severely.

Balaam rode on until the angel appeared again in a path between two vineyards. The donkey squeezed against a wall, and crushed Balaam's foot. So Balaam beat his donkey once more.

Then the angel blocked Balaam's path in a place where there was nowhere to turn. The donkey lay down, and Balaam beat her again. Then God gave the donkey the gift of speech.

'Why do you beat me?' the donkey said to Balaam. 'Would I have stopped if there hadn't been a good reason?'

Suddenly Balaam was able to see the angel in front of him.

'Why have you beaten your donkey?' asked the angel. 'She has saved your life! Listen to what God wants you to do. Go to Balak, but you must tell him only the words that God gives you to speak.'

71 BALAAM'S BLESSING

Balaam asked King Balak to build seven altars, prepare seven bulls and seven rams and sacrifice them on the altars.

Then Balaam went to a barren hill top to listen to God's message. Balaam brought the message to Balak.

'You brought me here to curse Jacob's descendants, the sons of Israel. How can I curse those whom God has blessed? These people are not like everyone else. They are a good people and I hope I may die as they do.'

Balak was very angry.

'I have brought you here to curse my enemies, not bless them!' he said.

'I can only say the words God gives me to say,' replied Balaam.

Again Balak prepared seven altars and again God gave Balaam the words to say.

'God does not lie. God keeps his promises. God brought this people out of Egypt and he will be with them and bless them,' said Balaam.

A third time Balak prepared his seven altars and a third time Balaam delivered God's blessing on his people.

'God saved his people from slavery in Egypt, and he will bless them with a land full of good things. God will make them strong against all their enemies and no one will be able to stand against them.'

Balak was furious! He sent Balaam away with no money for his trouble. Balaam left him with a warning.

'No amount of money would prevent me from giving you the words that God gave me. God has warned me that there will come a time in the future when one will come from Israel who is so strong that he will defeat your people.'

72 A HOLY NATION

After so many years in the desert, the Israelites were camped on the border of the promised land. It was time for Moses to remind them of all that God had done since their ancestors had left Egypt.

Moses warned them to live in a way that pleased God, following the ten commandments. He told them that God wanted them to be a special people who cared about others, who were generous and kind.

'When you enter Canaan,' Moses told them, 'you must help those among you who are poor. Share what you have and if you lend or borrow money, after seven years the debt will be cancelled. No one should suffer injustice among you. Be generous to one another, and God will bless you.

'You will be a great nation, and your enemies will be defeated,' Moses continued. 'You will have abundant harvests, plenty of water, and be blessed with many children. Other countries will watch and see that God has blessed you. But,' warned Moses, 'God will make you a special and holy nation only if you love him and obey his commandments. He has set before you life or death. Choose life, and live for a long time in the land he will give you.'

73 GOD CHOOSES JOSHUA

Moses was now an old man. He had served God well and led his people through many years in the desert. His brother and sister, Aaron and Miriam, had died long before.

So Moses spoke to the people one last time.

'I am 120 years old and I cannot lead you any more. God has told me that I will not cross the Jordan into the promised land. God himself will go with you and he will give you all that he has promised. Be strong and brave. God will go with you and you will never be alone.'

Then Moses laid his hands on Joshua in front of all the people.

'Be strong and full of courage. God has chosen you to lead his people into the promised land and you must take them there and divide the land between them.'

Moses blessed the people and then he climbed Mount Nebo. God showed Moses all the land that he would give to the Israelites.

'This is the land I promised to give to the descendants of Abraham, Isaac and Jacob,' God said.

Moses looked at the land and was content to die. He died in Moab and was buried there.

The Israelites mourned his death. They knew that Moses had spoken to God, face to face. He had done wonderful things, and he had spoken God's words to his people.

God's Spirit came to Joshua. He was wise and obedient and the Israelites listened to him.

74 RAHAB AND THE SPIES

Joshua prepared to enter Canaan by sending spies into the city of Jericho on the other side of the River Jordan.

The spies went secretly to a house built into the city walls and talked to Rahab, the woman who lived there. The king of Jericho was told that there were spies in Rahab's house, so he sent a message for her to hand them over.

Rahab hid the spies under the flax drying on her roof. Then she sent a message to the king saying that the spies had left earlier by the city gate.

Rahab watched as the king's men went in pursuit of the spies. When it was safe, she went to the men who were hiding and made a bargain with them.

'All my people know that your God dried up the waters of the Red Sea and saved you from the Egyptians. We know that he is with you now and will give you the city of Jericho. We are afraid because God is on your side. Promise me that you will help me and save my family when you come to capture the city.'

The spies agreed. They told her to hang a scarlet cord from her window in the city wall and to have her whole family there in the room when the Israelites came into the city. Then the spies went out through the window and down the city walls, escaping to hide in the hills.

75 CROSSING THE RIVER JORDAN

The spies brought Joshua news that the people of Jericho feared for their lives. God had gone before them to take the city.

Now Joshua had to cross the River Jordan with all the people.

'Today, everyone will know that I am with you, just as I was with Moses,' said God. He told Joshua how he would lead the people across the river.

At Joshua's command, the priests carried the ark into the river, and the people followed. Immediately, the waters that ran downstream stopped flowing. The priests stayed in the middle of the river, and the Israelites, men, women and children, crossed on dry land.

'Choose one man from each of the twelve tribes,' said God to Joshua. 'Tell them to take one stone each from the middle of the river bed, and to place them near where you camp tonight. Then your children and grandchildren will know what I have done for you.'

When all the people had crossed the river, the priests carrying the ark of the covenant walked to the other side too. Only then did the waters flow again.

No one wanted to fight against the Israelites after this. Everyone in Canaan heard what God had done for them.

76 VICTORY IN JERICHO

Joshua camped with the people outside Jericho. They celebrated the Passover and waited until God told them what to do next.

Then a man with a sword in his hand appeared in Joshua's path. Joshua knew he had been sent by God, and fell to his knees.

'I am the commander of God's army,' said the man. 'This is what you must do. Seven priests must lead you in a march around the city walls. The priests must walk in front of the ark, each carrying a trumpet, for six days. On the seventh day, they must march around the city walls seven times, blowing their trumpets. On the long trumpet blast, signal to the people to shout. Then the city walls will collapse.'

The gates of the city of Jericho stood before Joshua and his army, firmly closed against them.

For six days they marched as God had told them. On the seventh day, at the sound of the long trumpet blast, the people shouted, and the walls of Jericho crumbled and fell down.

Then the Israelites marched into the city. God had given them the victory. They found Rahab and her family and kept them safe as they had promised.

77 STOLEN SILVER AND GOLD

'Don't take anything for yourselves when we march into the city!' Joshua had warned his troops as they entered Jericho. 'Everything belongs to God.'

Achan found a beautiful robe, some silver and gold, and hid them secretly under his tent.

Joshua then sent 3000 soldiers into Ai to take the city. Spies had been sent in and reported that it could be defeated without the whole army in place. Yet the Israelites were defeated at Ai, and 36 soldiers were killed.

Joshua prayed to God.

'Why have you let us be defeated, Lord? We trusted you to help us.'

'Someone has disobeyed me,' God replied. 'They have stolen from Jericho and kept riches for themselves. Then they have lied about it.'

Joshua gathered the people. When Achan stood accused in front of him, Joshua challenged him.

'Tell me what you have done,' he said. 'Men died because of this. Hide nothing from me.'

Achan admitted that he had cheated and lied, and Joshua sent his men to find the stolen items. Then Achan was put to death for his disobedience.

78 VICTORY AT AI

God told Joshua that the time was right to attack the city of Ai.

'Don't be discouraged,' said God. 'This time, you will win the battle.'

Joshua chose his army.

'Half of you must go by night and hide on the far side of the city,' he said. 'In the morning, the rest of us will attack the city gates. The king of Ai will chase us, and we will lead his army away from the city. Then we can take Ai while it is not defended.'

Joshua and his army advanced. The king and his troops ran out to fight the Israelites as they had done before. Then they chased them as far as the desert.

God told Joshua to give the rest of the army the sign they had agreed and the rest of the army came from behind and burned the city to the ground. When the Israelites saw the smoke, they turned back to fight the soldiers of Ai who were now surrounded.

Joshua's men drove them into the desert. God had given them the victory.

79 THE PEACE TREATY

As Joshua took the Israelites further into Canaan, all the kings around grew afraid.

The people of Gibeon decided not to fight and lose. They preferred to make a pact with Israel. So they dressed in old clothes and loaded their donkeys with cracked wineskins and stale bread to deceive the Israelites.

'We have come from far away,' they lied. 'We want to make a peace treaty with you.'

Joshua and his leaders did not ask God what they should do. They made a peace treaty with the Gibeonites. When they realised that these men were their enemies, and lived in Canaan, they were angry.

'We will not break our promise,' said Joshua, 'but you must now work for us, cutting wood and carrying water for us.'

'Your God is a great God,' the Gibeonites told Joshua. 'We know that he has promised to give you this land and destroy everyone else who lives here. We wanted peace. We will work for you rather than die.'

80 THE SUN STANDS STILL

King Adonizedek from Jerusalem heard about the pact the Gibeonites had made with Joshua.

He feared what Joshua could do with their help so he joined forces with four other kings in Canaan.

'Come with me and let's attack Gibeon!' he said.

Once the attack had begun, the Gibeonites sent for help.

'Joshua! Come and rescue us! The Amorite kings want us dead!' the message reported. 'We are your servants. Help us!'

God spoke to Joshua.

'Don't be afraid. I will help you defeat the Amorites.'

So Joshua marched towards Gibeon and took the Amorites by surprise. As the enemy armies fled, God sent huge hailstones from the sky, which battered the enemy soldiers to death.

Then, in the middle of the day, Joshua prayed.

'Don't let the sun go down until we have the victory!' he said.

God answered him. The sun did not set until the battle was won.

81 THE BATTLE FOR CANAAN

As Joshua led the Israelites northwards, King Jabin of Hazor watched his progress.

'Come and fight these Israelites with me!' he said to his allies. They gathered a huge army, with horses and chariots, and set out to confront the Israelites.

When Joshua saw his enemies approaching, it seemed that they numbered more than the grains of sand on a beach.

'Don't be afraid,' said God to Joshua. 'By this time tomorrow you will have defeated them.'

Joshua trusted God and made a surprise attack at Merom Pond. By disabling the horses and burning the chariots, Joshua was able to defeat his enemies.

Joshua led the Israelites in victory over 31 kings. Canaan was theirs at last. Now the Israelites could enjoy the land that God had promised them.

82 THE TWELVE TRIBES OF ISRAEL

The Israelites had the land of Canaan before them. Joshua's last task was to divide the land between all the tribes of Israel.

Jacob had had twelve sons. The sons of Levi were priests and did not take a share of the land; the land that should have been Joseph's was divided between his two sons. So it was that the land was divided into twelve parts.

Now, at last, the people could stop wandering and receive their inheritance, their new home.

'Don't forget all that God has done for you,' said Joshua. 'Remember to love him and keep his laws and he will never forget his promises to you. You will live safely in the land as long as you don't marry the people on your borders or worship their gods. The Lord is our God. He has made an agreement with us as he did with Abraham, Isaac and Jacob.'

83 CALEB'S REWARD

Many years had passed since Joshua and Caleb had been spies sent into Canaan by Moses. They alone had been allowed to see the day when the people would settle in the land God had promised; they alone had believed God would keep his promises even when the other spies would not trust him. Joshua and Caleb had seen God help them conquer their enemies. Now it was time for Caleb to receive the reward Moses had promised.

'Forty-five years ago, Moses promised that I would have a share of the land to pass on to my children,' Caleb said to Joshua. 'Now I am 85! God has kept me fit and well for this day. Please give me the hill country of Hebron. I know the people there are unfriendly but I am still strong and God will take care of me.'

Joshua blessed his old friend, Caleb. He knew that he loved God and trusted him still. He gave Caleb the area of Hebron as his special reward.

84 JOSHUA SAYS GOODBYE

There was peace in the land of Canaan.

Joshua lived to be 110 years old. One day he called together the leaders of the people to say goodbye.

'I am old and must soon die,' he said to them. 'You have seen how God has kept his promises and given us this land. Be strong and always keep God's laws. Keep yourselves separate from the other nations around you. Love God with all your hearts.'

Then Joshua gave the people a message from God.

'Remember that I brought Abraham out of a land where they worshipped other gods and gave him Isaac; I gave to Isaac sons, Esau and Jacob. When Jacob's family were in Egypt, I sent Moses and Aaron to lead them out of slavery. Then I brought you across the River Jordan and helped you defeat all the Amorites and the other people who lived in Canaan. Now this land is yours.'

Then Joshua said, 'Choose today which god you will trust and worship. As for me and all my family, we will serve the Lord.'

Then the people promised to trust and obey God alone. Joshua took a large stone and placed it under an oak tree at Shechem.

'This stone will be here always as a reminder of your promise to serve the living God.'

Joshua died and the people buried him. Aaron's son, Eleazar, the priest, died and was buried also. And the bones of Joseph were brought from Egypt and buried at Shechem.

85 THE PEOPLE FORGET GOD'S LAWS

It was not long before a whole generation of Israelites who loved and served the Lord had died. Their children quickly forgot what they had been taught. They chose not to follow God's laws but worshipped the gods of the people around them.

Soon the Israelites began to marry into the nations round about them. They were no longer God's separate people. They worshipped Baal and Ashtoreth, the gods the Canaanites believed gave them rain to grow their crops and large families to carry on their family name.

The Israelites lived in ways that angered God and they forgot the promises their ancestors had made.

Without God's help, raiders plundered their lands and they were defeated in battle. Then Cushan-Rishathaim, king of Aram, overpowered them and made them his subjects for eight years.

The Israelites were no longer free. They began to call out to God for help once more.

86 CALEB'S NEPHEW TO THE RESCUE

God had compassion on his people; he did not forget them.

God brought them a judge, Othniel, who was Caleb's nephew. The Spirit of the Lord came to Othniel, and he was able to guide the people back to God's laws.

Othniel went to war against Cushan-Rishathaim and, with God's help, he overpowered the king of Aram so that there was once more peace in the land of Canaan.

For 40 years Othniel guided the Israelites but when he died, the people returned to their old ways. They rebelled against God's laws and did wicked deeds that angered God once more.

Then God allowed Eglon, the king of Moab, to make a pact with Israel's enemies, the Ammonites and Amalekites. Eglon gathered an army and captured Jericho, also called the City of Palms.

The Israelites were once more overpowered and for 18 years they were Eglon's subjects.

Then, as before, they called to God for help.

87 EHUD, THE LEFT-HANDED JUDGE

God heard the cries of his people and he sent Ehud, from the tribe of Benjamin, to rescue them.

When King Eglon demanded a tribute from the Israelites, the people chose Ehud to take it to the king.

Ehud, a left-handed man, made a long double-edged sword and strapped it to his right thigh, underneath his tunic.

First Ehud bowed before the king, and gave him the tribute. He dismissed the men who had helped him carry the gifts and then whispered, 'I have a secret message for you, your majesty.'

Eglon was intrigued and sent his attendants away. He invited Ehud to enter the upper room of his summer palace, not realising that Ehud was armed.

Ehud approached the king, who was a very large, fat man.

'I have a message from God for you,' he said. Ehud reached for his sword and plunged it into the king's belly, killing him. Quietly, Ehud left the room, locked the doors behind him, and made his escape.

When Ehud reached the hill country, he blew his trumpet. The Israelites rushed down the hills.

'Follow me!' cried Ehud as he led the people into battle. 'God has helped us defeat the people of Moab!'

Then there was peace in the land for 80 years.

88 DEBORAH AND BARAK

After Ehud died, the Israelites stopped following God's ways again. It was not long before God let one of the kings who lived in Canaan oppress them.

King Jabin had a large and fierce army under the command of a man called Sisera. He equipped his troops with 900 iron chariots, and for 20 years he oppressed Israel. The Israelites suffered and cried out to God.

Deborah, the wife of Lappidoth, led Israel at this time. She was a prophet who served the living God, and people would come to her for wisdom when they had disputes to settle.

God spoke to Deborah about King Jabin. Then she sent for a warrior called Barak.

'I have a message for you from God,' Deborah told Barak. 'You must take 10,000 troops and march to Mount Tabor. God will lure Sisera and King Jabin's army toward the River Kishon. Then they will be trapped, and you can defeat them.'

Barak was frightened.

'I cannot do this alone,' he said. 'You must come with me.'

Deborah was disappointed by Barak's response, but she agreed.

'Be warned!' she said. 'Because you have not acted on God's instructions, a woman will have the victory over Sisera.'

89 JAEL'S TENT PEG

When Sisera heard that Barak was leading an attack, he gathered his army and 900 chariots by the River Kishon and waited.

Barak went up to Mount Tabor with his troops, where they were safe from the chariots.

'Attack!' signalled Deborah to Barak. 'This is what God wants us to do. Today we will defeat our enemies.'

Barak's troops charged down the hillside, attacking Sisera's army, slashing with their swords. Sisera abandoned his chariot and ran. He knew that his army could not win. He headed towards some tents belonging to a man called Heber.

Heber's wife, Jael, saw Sisera. She knew who he was. 'Don't be afraid,' she said. 'No one will find you here in my tent.' Sisera went inside and asked for a drink. Jael gave him milk and hid him under some covers.

'Keep watch!' he pleaded. 'If someone comes looking for me, don't tell them I am here!' He was exhausted, and fell fast asleep.

Jael did not keep watch. She was on God's side. Instead, she drove a tent peg through his head and killed him.

Barak charged through Heber's camp, looking for Sisera.

'Look no further,' said Jael. 'I will show you the man you have come for.'

Barak saw the body of his enemy, killed by a woman, just as Deborah had prophesied. King Jabin was unable to fight back.

'Praise the Lord!' sang Deborah and Barak. 'He has defeated our enemies.'

90 THE CAMEL RIDERS

The Israelites enjoyed peace for another 40 years, but then they forgot all the things that God had done for them. They went back to their evil ways and God left them to the mercy of the Midianites.

The Israelites hid in the mountains and were afraid to stay in the open. The Midianites would wait until the Israelites had grown their crops, then they would swoop down on camels and spoil the land or steal what they had grown. As a result the Israelites were weak from hunger and frightened for their lives. They lived like this for seven years.

When the Israelites cried to the Lord for help, he sent them a prophet.

'We have disobeyed God!' he warned the people. 'That is why we are being attacked by our enemies.'

91 GIDEON, THE RELUCTANT HERO

Gideon, the son of Joash, was trying to thresh wheat in secret, out of sight of the Midianites.

An angel came to sit under an oak tree and watched him.

'God is with you, mighty warrior!' the angel said to Gideon.

'Then why are we in so much trouble?' Gideon answered. 'God brought our ancestors out of Egypt only to let us die under the Midianites!'

'You can change that,' said the angel. 'God wants you to save Israel from the Midianites.'

'Why would God send me? I am no one! I belong to the smallest clan in my tribe; I am the least in my family!'

'You can do this because I will be with you,' said the angel. 'We will save Israel together.'

Gideon was amazed. 'Please show me a sign,' said Gideon. 'Prove to me that this is not just a dream.'

Gideon rushed home and returned with food as an offering.

'Put the food on a rock,' said the angel.

Gideon did so and the angel touched it with his staff. The food caught alight; and the angel vanished.

Then Gideon believed that he had been in the company of an angel sent by God, and he was afraid.

'You have nothing to fear, Gideon. You will not die.'

92 GIDEON AND THE SHEEPSKIN

That night Gideon prayed for God's help.

'I need to be sure that you want me to save Israel,' said Gideon. 'I will put a sheepskin on the ground this evening. In the morning, if the sheepskin is wet and the ground dry, I will know that you want me to lead Israel.'

In the morning Gideon squeezed the sheepskin. It was wet, but the ground all around was dry. God had answered his prayer.

It was not enough.

'Don't be angry with me, Lord, but I must be sure. Let me put the sheepskin out again, only this time let the ground be wet and the sheepskin dry.'

In the morning the ground was covered with dew, and the sheepskin was dry. Gideon had his answer. God had chosen him, the least of his family, to lead his people against his enemies.

93 GIDEON'S SMALL ARMY

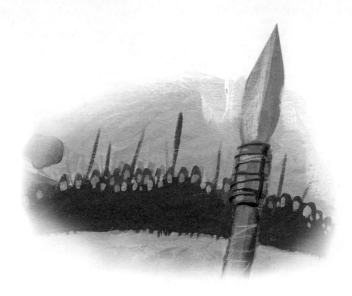

The Israelite army gathered together and made camp.

'You have too many soldiers,' said God to Gideon. 'When the battle is won, the people will say that they did it in their own strength. Tell anyone who is afraid that they may go home.'

That day, 22,000 men went home. Only 10,000 remained.

'There are still too many,' said God. 'Ask the men to go to the river and drink.'

Some of the men knelt down to drink, while others stood up and lapped the water out of their hands like dogs.

'I will use the men who stood up and lapped the water,' said God. 'Send the others home.'

Gideon obeyed God. He now had an army of just 300 men to fight the Midianites.

94 BATTLE BY NIGHT

'It is time to defeat your enemies!' said God. 'First, go down to the enemy camp and listen. Then you will not be afraid to attack.'

Gideon went silently to the enemy camp. There were tens of thousands of men and more camels than grains of sand on the seashore. Gideon had just 300 men.

'I've had a terrible dream!' Gideon heard someone say. 'A huge barley loaf rolled into our camp and made the tent collapse.'

'Then God will surely help Gideon win,' said another voice.

Gideon thanked God for what he had heard. He returned and woke his men.

'Come! God has already won the battle!' he told them.

Gideon divided the men into three groups, and gave each man a trumpet and a burning torch covered by an empty jar. In the darkness, the Israelites surrounded the enemy camp. At Gideon's signal, he and his men blew their trumpets and smashed the jars.

'For the Lord and for Gideon!' they cried.

The Midianites and the Amalekites were terrified. They stumbled and fell upon each other in the darkness. They killed each other with their swords. Those who remained fled to the hills.

It was just as God had said. God had rescued the Israelites once again.

95 ABIMELECH KILLS HIS BROTHERS

The people went to Gideon and asked him to rule over them.

'The Lord God will rule over you. You need no other,' he said. 'Neither I nor my sons will be your ruler.' One of Gideon's sons had other ideas.

Gideon had married many wives and had many children. One of his sons was called Abimelech. His mother was one of Gideon's slaves. Abimelech went to his mother's home town of Shechem after Gideon's death and spoke to his relatives.

'Choose me as your leader. Don't let any of my half-brothers rule over you.'

Abimelech's relatives agreed and he hired a band of men to follow him. Then he went to his father's home town and killed all his half-brothers. Only the youngest, Jotham, escaped. Then Abimelech returned to Shechem and the people crowned him king.

When Jotham heard this, he went to Shechem and climbed to the top of Mount Gerizim.

'Remember what my father did for you!' he cried. 'Now think about what you have done to his family!'

Abimelech ruled Israel for three years, but God had seen the evil thing he had done.

96 ABIMELECH'S PUNISHMENT

A man called Gaal came to Shechem. Before long he had a number of friends and supporters.

'Follow me and we will defeat Abimelech and his army,' he said.

'Gaal is stirring up trouble,' Zebul, the govenor of the city, warned Abimelech. 'Make a dawn attack and destroy him and his followers.'

As Abimelech approached Shechem, Gaal and his friends fought bravely, but were driven out of the city. The next day, when Abimelech attacked Shechem again, the people hid in the stronghold of the temple. Abimelech surrounded it with burning branches, so they were all killed.

As Abimelech marched on, the people locked themselves in a strong tower. Abimelech made his way towards the entrance to burn it as he had before, but this time one of the women saw what Abimelech was trying to do. She lifted a heavy millstone, and flung it down on top of him. It landed on Abimelech's head and cracked his skull.

'Kill me with your sword!' the wounded Abimelech begged his servant. 'Let them not say that a woman killed me.'

The servant obeyed. When the Israelites saw what had happened, they left the city. God had punished Abimelech for the terrible things he had done.

97 JEPHTHAH'S RASH PROMISE

The Israelites continued to disobey God, and the Ammonites oppressed them.

The elders of Gilead went to Jephthah, who was a great warrior, and asked him to be their leader.

'If God helps me defeat the Ammonites, will I still be your leader?' asked Jephthah.

'We promise,' they replied.

First Jephthah sent a peaceful message to the Ammonite king.

'What have we done to make you oppress us?' he asked.

'You took my land when God brought you out of Egypt,' said the king. Jephthah knew this was not true.

'We only took the land of those who would not let us pass through. Then we took the land that God gave to us. We have lived here now for hundreds of years. If you really had any claim on the land, why make it now?' he asked.

Then Jephthah prayed foolishly to God.

'I will make a bargain with you. If you help me defeat my enemies, I will sacrifice the first thing I see when I return home!'

Jephthah led the Israelite army into victory. Then he went home. The first thing he saw was his only daughter, dancing. When Jephthah saw her, he remembered what he had promised God. He tore his clothes and wept. He knew that he had made a promise to God that he could not break.

98 THE BIRTH OF SAMSON

After Jephthah died, the people returned to their old ways. This time they were attacked by the Philistines, who then ruled over them for 40 years.

During this time God sent an angel to a childless woman, the wife of a man called Manoah.

'I know you have no children,' said the angel, 'but God will give you a son. He will save Israel from the Philistines. You must drink no wine before his birth and when he is born you must let his hair grow long, as a sign that he has been dedicated to God.'

The woman was amazed and she told her husband. Manoah prayed to God to send the angel again so that they could be sure to do all that God asked of them. The angel came again and repeated all he had said, and Manoah realised that God had blessed them with a special task.

Some months later, the woman gave birth to a son and called him Samson. God blessed the child and prepared him for the work he had to do.

99 SAMSON'S RIDDLE

When Samson grew up, he wanted to marry a Philistine woman.

His parents set off to make the wedding arrangements. Samson followed afterwards. As Samson walked through a vineyard, a young lion bounded towards him, ready to attack. God filled Samson with his Spirit and gave him amazing strength. He grappled with the lion, killing it with his bare hands.

Some time later, Samson returned to the vineyard. Bees had made a nest within the lion's carcass and there was honey inside. So during the wedding feast, Samson told his Philistine companions a riddle.

'Out of the eater, something to eat; out of the strong, something sweet. Tell me the answer to my riddle within seven days, and I will give you a prize. If not, you must reward me.'

The Philistines had no idea how to solve the riddle so they made Samson's new wife find out the answer. She begged Samson to tell her the secret of the riddle and then she told them.

'What is sweeter than honey? What is stronger than a lion?' they cried.

Samson knew he had been deceived. He wanted revenge.

100 SAMSON'S REVENGE

Samson went from the wedding feast and brought back the prize he had promised to give the Philistines. He left to return to his father's house afterwards. His father-in-law assumed he did not want his daughter, so he gave Samson's wife to another man.

When Samson returned to see his wife, he found that she was no longer his. In his anger, he took revenge on the Philistines.

He went out and caught 300 jackals and tied their tails together in pairs. Then he fastened a flaming torch to every pair of tails and let them loose in the cornfields.

The Philistines soon came looking for Samson. They sent men from Judah to capture him.

Samson allowed himself to be tied up by the men, but as soon as the Philistines came towards him, God gave him enormous strength. Samson broke through the ropes as if through butter. Then he used the jaw bone of a donkey to kill 1000 of his enemies.

Then Samson fell to his knees dying of thirst. He prayed to God to give him water after his victory, and God caused a spring to open up so that he could drink.

Samson led the Israelites against the Philistines for 20 years.

101 DELILAH BETRAYS SAMSON

The Philistines hated Samson but they could do nothing because God had given him such enormous strength. When Samson fell in love with Delilah, however, they saw their chance.

'Find out the secret of Samson's strength,' they said to her, 'and we will reward you.'

'Tell me the secret of your strength,' she whispered to him one night.

'Tie me with seven new bowstrings, and I will be as weak as any man,' Samson replied.

The Philistines brought Delilah the bowstrings, and while they hid in the room, she used them to tie Samson while he slept.

'The Philistines are here!' she screamed. Samson leapt up, and the strings snapped under his strength.

'Show me you trust me. Tell me your secret.' she tried again.

'You need new ropes,' he replied. 'Then I will be weak.'

This time Samson snapped the ropes as if they were thread.

'Weave on to the loom the seven braids of my hair,' said Samson, the next time she asked. This time he broke the loom.

Delilah continued to nag Samson every day. Eventually he could stand it no longer. 'If my head is shaved, I will lose my strength.'

Samson was asleep when the Philistines shaved the seven braids on his head. Samson's strength vanished. His enemies blinded him and put him in prison. He could not fight back.

102 SAMSON DEFEATS HIS ENEMIES

The Philistines were delighted that at last they had captured their enemy. They organised a celebration to thank their god Dagon for their success.

'Let Samson entertain us!' cried the people.

All the Philistine rulers were there; the temple was filled with the laughter of people of all ages, including 3000 on the flat roof. They had not noticed that Samson's hair had begun to grow again.

Samson could no longer see. He asked the servant who guided him to put him between the pillars of the temple.

'Remember me, Lord God,' prayed Samson, 'and give me strength once more. Punish the Philistines, and let me die as I have lived, destroying the enemies of your people.'

Samson pushed at the pillars with all his might. God answered his prayer and gave him back his strength. The giant pillars toppled, pulling the walls inwards and bringing the roof crashing to the ground.

Samson had destroyed the Philistine temple, and with it, thousands of Philistines. He had died in the attempt, but killed more of his enemies by his death than he had in his lifetime.

103 ELIMELECH'S FAMILY SETTLES IN MOAB

There was a famine in Israel during the time of the judges.

Elimelech took his wife Naomi and left his home near Bethlehem with his sons, Mahlon and Kilion. They went to Moab to find food.

Elimelech died in Moab. Mahlon and Kilion married and the family settled there for about ten years. Then Naomi's sons died too and the three women were left alone.

Naomi heard that the famine was now over in Israel and decided to return to Bethlehem.

'Stay here and go back to your mothers,' Naomi told her sons' widows. 'I will go back alone.'

Orpah went home. Ruth clung to her mother-in-law.

'I will never leave you,' she said. 'Your country will be my country and your people, my people. Your God will become my God and I will be buried where you are buried.'

Naomi saw that Ruth was serious, and so the two women went on to Bethlehem, where they arrived at the beginning of the barley harvest.

104 RUTH WORKS IN THE FIELDS

With no one to provide for them, Naomi and Ruth were hungry.

'I will pick up the leftover grain in the fields,' Ruth told Naomi.

God blessed Ruth, and she found herself working in the fields belonging to Boaz, a relative of Elimelech. She worked hard, and Boaz asked his workers who she was.

'She is Naomi's daughter-in-law,' the man replied. 'She came from Moab with Naomi even though her husband had died.'

Boaz went over to talk to Ruth.

'Stay and gather grain in my fields,' he said, 'and take some water whenever you are thirsty.'

'Why are you being so good to me?' Ruth asked.

'I have heard of your kindness to Naomi,' he replied. 'May God now bless you and reward you for your loyalty to her.'

Boaz provided Ruth with food that day and there was enough for her to take some home to Naomi, as well as the barley Ruth had picked up. Boaz had made sure that plenty was left for her.

Naomi was amazed at the amount she had gathered.

'Where did you go?' she asked. 'Someone has surely been kind to you.'

Ruth told Naomi about the kindness of the landowner. 'His name is Boaz,' she added.

'He is a relative of ours!' exclaimed Naomi. 'You must go to his fields again tomorrow.'

105 RUTH AND BOAZ

Ruth worked in Boaz's fields until the end of the harvest, and she and Naomi did not go hungry. At the end of that time, Naomi spoke to Ruth about her future.

'It's my duty to try to find a better home for you,' she said. 'We know that Boaz has been kind to you, and we are also related to him. It is our custom that if a man dies leaving a young wife, a relative should marry her to care for his family.'

'What must I do?' asked Ruth. 'Tell me and I will do it.'

Ruth did all Naomi told her. Ruth went to the threshing floor where Boaz had been celebrating the end of the harvest. She lay down at his feet and waited. When he woke in the night, he was surprised.

'Who's there?' he asked.

Ruth told him why she had come.

'I will look after you,' said Boaz kindly, 'but there is another relative who should be asked first. If he is happy to let you go, I will take care of you and Naomi.'

When Ruth returned home, she told Naomi all that had happened. Then together they waited.

106 NAOMI'S GRANDSON

Boaz went to the town gate and found Naomi's relative. In front of the elders of the people, Boaz asked him if he wanted to buy Elimelech's land, marry Ruth and raise children for her dead husband, Mahlon. The man decided that he could not do it, and offered the opportunity to Boaz.

Boaz was happy. He married Ruth and God blessed them all. Some time later, Naomi found herself not only happy in Boaz's household but proudly looking after her first grandchild.

'Everything was taken from me, but God gave me Ruth, who was better than all that was taken away. Now I have Obed, too, my grandson, and God has blessed me.'

Obed grew up to have a son called Jesse, who himself had eight sons. The youngest son was called David.

107 HANNAH'S SORROW

Every year Elkanah and his two wives, Hannah and Peninnah, went to Shiloh to worship God and make a special sacrifice.

Peninnah had many children but although Hannah longed to have a baby of her own, she had none. Peninnah often teased Hannah, until Hannah cried so much she couldn't eat.

One year, Hannah went to the place of worship and poured out all her sorrow.

'Lord God,' she prayed in her heart, 'if you will answer my prayer and let me give birth to a son, then I promise to give him back to you, to serve you all his life. Please hear and help me!'

When Eli, the priest, saw Hannah's lips moving but heard no sound, he thought she had been drinking and rebuked her. When Hannah told him that she was unhappy and had prayed to God, he was kind.

'May God answer your prayer and bless you,' he said.

Hannah returned home. God did answer her prayer and blessed her. Before long she found that she was expecting a baby. She gave birth to a son and called him Samuel.

108 HANNAH KEEPS HER PROMISE

Hannah cared for her baby son for several years and she loved him dearly. Then Hannah took Samuel to the place of worship in Shiloh and went to Eli the priest.

'Do you remember the unhappy woman who came here and asked God to bless her?' she asked him. 'I am that woman; but I am no longer unhappy. God has blessed me with a baby son, and now I must keep my promise. My son must live here in the temple and learn how to serve God.'

Every year after that Hannah came to visit Samuel and brought him a new robe that she had made for him.

Eli asked God to bless Hannah so she would have other children, and in time she had three more sons and two daughters.

Eli had two sons of his own called Hophni and Phinehas. They had grown up and become priests like their father. Both were selfish men who broke God's rules and did not serve God well.

Eli was sad when he saw how his sons behaved and he warned them that God would be angry with them. Hophni and Phinehas did not listen to him.

Samuel became Eli's helper. God watched as Samuel grew up, and he blessed him.

109 GOD SPEAKS IN THE NIGHT

As Eli grew older, he depended more and more on Samuel's help.

One night, while the golden lampstand was still alight, and everyone was asleep, God called to Samuel.

Samuel woke at the sound of the voice but he did not know who it was. He got up and went to Eli.

'Here I am!' said Samuel. 'You called me!'

'No, I didn't call,' said Eli. 'Go back to sleep.'

Before long Samuel heard the voice calling him again.

He went again to Eli.

'I didn't call you,' said Eli. 'Go back to your bed.'

When Samuel heard the voice a third time, Eli understood.

'God is calling you,' said Eli. 'Go back to bed. If the voice calls again, reply, "Speak, Lord, for your servant is listening."'

God called Samuel again and he answered.

From that day God spoke to Samuel and Samuel learned to listen and to act on all that God asked him to do.

Eli and all the people saw that God was with Samuel and that he spoke with God's authority. Samuel was the prophet that God had sent to help his people.

110 THE DEATH OF ELI

When the Israelites went into battle with the Philistines and were defeated, they returned to camp and decided to take with them the ark of the covenant.

Hophni and Phinehas went with the ark. They believed that if the ark was with them in battle, God was with them too.

The Philistines saw how brave the ark made the Israelite soldiers. They began to tremble and be afraid. These were the same people whose God had brought them out of Egypt!

Both sides engaged in battle, but although the ark was there, God was not with the Israelites that day. Hophni and Phinehas died along with 30,000 men; and the Philistines captured the ark of the covenant and carried it away with them.

A young man ran from the battle line to tell the Israelites what had happened. When he told the people, they were all very afraid. Eli was sitting at the gate, waiting. He was very frail.

'What has happened?' Eli asked. 'Tell me everything.'

'Our people have fled from the enemy; we have lost a great many men in battle. Your sons are dead and the Philistines have captured the ark of the covenant.'

Eli was greatly shocked and fell down dead at the news. His daughter-in-law, the wife of Phinehas, was expecting a baby at that time. She went into labour and gave birth to a son. She named him Ichabod, which means 'no glory', because she believed that God had left his people.

111 THE ARK IN DAGON'S TEMPLE

The Philistines took the ark of the covenant to Ashdod where they put it next to their god, Dagon, in the temple there.

The next day, the people went into the temple and found that the statue of their god had fallen on its face in front of the ark of the covenant. They lifted the statue and put it back again but by next morning, it had not only fallen again, but its head and hands had broken off.

Then there was a plague on the people of Ashdod and they were overrun with rats. They suffered terribly and began to see that the ark of the covenant could not stay in their town. They moved it to Gath, but then there was a plague on the people of Gath. They moved it to Ekron, and the same thing happened there.

'Take the ark away!' cried the people. 'Send it back to the Israelites or we will all die!'

So the ark of the covenant was put on a cart with some gifts of gold and hitched up to two cows. They put it on the road and set it on its way.

'If the cows go straight to the country of the Israelites, we will know their God has sent these plagues,' they said. 'If not, then all of our suffering has just been an act of chance.'

The cart went in the direction of the Israelites' country.

The Israelites rejoiced to see the ark returned to them! They sacrificed the cows that had pulled the cart, and worshipped God.

112 SAMUEL LEADS GOD'S PEOPLE

After Eli's death, Samuel waited to see when the people would call out to God again. When he thought they were sorry that they had worshipped other gods, and were ready to try again to follow God's ways, he called them all together.

'If you are ready to return to God and love him with all your hearts, then you must destroy all the idols you own and promise to serve God alone,' he said. 'Then God will drive out the Philistines.'

The people destroyed all the images of Baal and the Ashtoreths they had collected, and worshipped God once more.

Then Samuel told them he would pray for them.

'We have sinned, Lord, and we are sorry. Please forgive us. Be our God as you were the God of our ancestors.'

When the Philistines threatened to attack the Israelites at Mizpah, the people were afraid.

Samuel offered sacrifices to God and kept on praying.

God heard the prayers of his people. He sent thunder, which threw the Philistines into confusion and gave the Israelites the opportunity to attack and defeat their enemy.

Samuel set a stone in the ground and called it Ebenezer to mark the fact that God had helped his people there.

From that time on, Samuel became Israel's leader, and he judged the people wisely.

113 THE PEOPLE WANT A KING

Samuel grew to be old and, although he had sons, they did not listen to God or obey him, just as Eli's sons had not.

'We want a king like all the other nations!' cried Israel's elders as they stood before Samuel. 'You are old and there is no good man to follow you who serves God.'

Samuel was sad and he was angry with the people. He prayed to God.

'Listen to the people,' said God. 'It is not that they are rejecting you; they are rejecting me. A king cannot bring them what they want, but they are just as stubborn as their ancestors before them. They must learn this for themselves. They can have a king but he will bring them great unhappiness.'

Samuel warned the people as God told him to, but they refused to listen.

114 THE FIRST KING OF ISRAEL

Kish had a son called Saul, a tall, handsome young man. Kish's donkeys had wandered off into the hills so he sent Saul to find them.

After several days, they had still not found the donkeys. Saul decided they should return.

'Soon my father will stop worrying about his donkeys and start worrying about his son!' he told his servant.

'There is a man of God nearby. Perhaps we could ask him?'

God had already told Samuel that he had chosen the man who would be Israel's future king. When Samuel saw Saul walking towards him, he knew that this was the man God had chosen.

'We are looking for the seer, God's prophet,' Saul said.

'You have found him,' Samuel answered. 'Come and eat with me and tomorrow I have something important to tell you. Don't worry any more about your lost donkeys. They have been found.'

The following day, Saul and his servant prepared to leave with the donkeys. Samuel told Saul to order his servant to go on a while without him.

When they were alone, Samuel took some oil and anointed Saul, the first king of Israel.

'God will change you and give you power to be the person who will be Israel's king. Don't be afraid; God will help you.'

115 SAUL, THE WARRIOR KING

Saul returned to his family with his donkeys but he told no one about God's plans for him.

Then Samuel called all the people together.

'You have rejected God who brought your ancestors out of Egypt,' he said. 'You have chosen to have a king rule over you instead. Now come to see whom God has chosen to be king.'

Samuel went through the tribes of Israel until Benjamin was chosen; he went through the families until the family of Kish was chosen and then Saul, his son.

'Long live the king!' shouted God's people when Samuel presented their new leader to them.

Meanwhile, the Ammonites attacked the Israelite city of Jabesh. The people of Jabesh wanted to make peace with them.

'We will make peace on one condition,' agreed the Ammonites. 'We will blind all your inhabitants in one eye.'

When the Israelites heard this, they were afraid. God gave Saul the power to lead them. He led them in a surprise attack.

Then the people hailed Saul as their warrior king. He had helped them to victory and made them brave in battle. The Israelites had what they had asked for: a king, like the other nations.

116
JONATHAN FIGHTS THE PHILISTINES

God gave Samuel rules so that Saul would be a good king. At first Saul listened and did what God told him to do. As time went on, Saul started to act without God's blessing.

'You have disobeyed God,' Samuel told Saul. 'Now he will look for another king, a man who listens to him and obeys him.'

One day Saul and his army were preparing for a battle with the Philistines, who continued to raid Israel. Saul's son, Jonathan, left the group unnoticed, taking his armour-bearer with him.

'Let's find out what the Philistines are doing,' Jonathan said to him. 'God may bless us and give us victory.'

They climbed up into the rocky mountains.

'We'll let the enemy see us,' Jonathan told his armour-bearer. 'If they say, "We're coming to get you!" we'll stay here. If they say, "Come here and get us!" we'll know God will help us defeat them.'

As soon as the Philistines saw Jonathan, they dared him to come and fight. Jonathan climbed over the rocks, his servant following behind. The Philistine army fell back as Jonathan approached, and soon Jonathan and his armour-bearer had killed many of their enemies. Then God sent an earth tremor causing the Philistines to panic and kill each other with their own swords.

God had given the Israelites victory through Jonathan.

117 JESSE'S YOUNGEST SON

Saul continued to act even when it was the opposite of what God told him to do. He gave in when the people wanted to take plunder from their enemies and this made Samuel grieve.

'God wants your obedience, not your sacrifices on altars,' Samuel told him. 'God has warned me that because you have rejected his guidance, he is rejecting you as king.'

'Fill your horn with oil,' said God one day. 'I have chosen the man who will be king after Saul. Go to Bethlehem and invite a man called Jesse to a feast.'

When Samuel saw Jesse's eldest son, he felt sure that he must be God's choice, but God said no.

'I have not chosen him, Samuel. You see what a person looks like on the outside, but I see what is inside their heart.'

When Samuel had met seven of Jesse's sons, and none of them was the one God had chosen, Samuel asked whether Jesse had any more sons.

'My youngest son is looking after the sheep,' replied Jesse.

They sent for David and brought him to the feast. When Samuel saw him, God told him that this was his chosen king. So Samuel anointed David with oil in front of all his family, and God's Spirit filled him.

118 THE KING'S UNHAPPY MOODS

Once God had stopped blessing Saul, the king suffered from depression and his mind was full of bad, unhappy thoughts.

'Let us find someone who plays soothing music to help you,' his servants offered.

Saul agreed and asked them to find someone.

'One of Jesse's sons plays well,' suggested a servant. 'He is a fine young man, and he loves the living God.'

So King Saul sent a message to Jesse to bring his son to him.

Jesse loaded a donkey with gifts of bread and wine and a young goat and took David to see the king.

David played his harp whenever the king suffered from his unhappy moods, and Saul was happy to have David there. He asked Jesse to let him stay and become one of his armour-bearers.

119 THE SHEPHERD'S SONG

David made up songs and sang these when he played his harp.

'You, Lord, are my shepherd. I will never be in need.

'You let me rest in fields of green grass.

'You lead me where there are streams of cool water, and you give me peace.

'You lead me along the right paths, because you can only do what is right.

'I may walk through valleys as dark as death, but I won't be afraid, because you are with me and care for me, as a shepherd makes his sheep feel safe.

'You treat me as an honoured guest at a feast, while my enemies watch.

'You fill my cup until it overflows.

'Your kindness and love will always be with me every day of my life, and I will live for ever in your house, Lord.'

120 THE GIANT'S CHALLENGE

The Israelites were gathered on one hill; the Philistines were on the other. The Philistine champion, Goliath, was in the valley below. His head was protected by a bronze helmet; his body by bronze armour; his legs were protected by bronze greaves and he carried a bronze javelin on his back. In his hand was a spear with a heavy iron point. Day by day, Goliath asked for a man to fight him.

The Israelites were terrified. No one would go.

One day David brought food supplies to the Israelite camp. He heard Goliath shouting and saw that no one stood up to him.

'How dare he challenge us!' said David to the men around him. 'We have the living God on our side.'

King Saul sent for David.

'If our army will not fight this giant,' David said, 'I will go.'

'This giant is a professional fighter,' Saul said. 'You are a boy.'

'I look after my father's sheep,' answered David, 'and God saves me from the lion and bear. He can surely save me from this Philistine.'

David tried the king's armour but it was too big and heavy. So he took his sling and chose five small stones from the stream.

'You have sword and spear and javelin but I have the living God on my side! Today the whole world will know that there is a God in Israel.'

David slipped a stone into his sling and whirled it around his head. The stone shot through the air and hit Goliath's forehead. He sank to the ground and the Israelite army cheered. Their enemy's champion was dead and his army had run away.

121 SAUL,
THE JEALOUS KING

After David had defeated Goliath, he became firm friends with Jonathan, King Saul's son, and married one of Saul's daughters.

Saul gave David many things to do, and he saw that God blessed him in everything. Saul then promoted him to a position of great authority in his army and David was both popular with the people and successful.

Saul watched all that happened. Soon Saul felt jealous that David was everything he thought he should be as king.

One day when David was playing his harp, Saul was gripped with such anger and jealousy towards David that he picked up his spear and hurled it at him. Saul missed and David was not hurt, but Saul had hoped to kill him.

Then Saul sent David away. He could not bear to have him close by. Saul saw that God blessed David whenever he led the Israelites into battle with the Philistines.

122 JONATHAN'S WARNING

Jonathan went to his friend David one day.

'David, you must hide,' warned Jonathan. 'My father wants to kill you. I will try to persuade him that you mean him no harm.'

King Saul listened to Jonathan and promised not to kill David, but at the next opportunity, he threw his spear at him again. Once more David escaped.

'I don't understand why your father wants to kill me,' said David to Jonathan at one of their secret meetings. 'How can I trust him and be safe?'

'He tells me everything,' said Jonathan, 'and you are my closest friend. I will not let him hurt you. Now, he will expect you at the New Moon Feast. If it is safe for you to come, I will send you a sign. If your life is in danger, then you will also know.'

When everyone except David came to the feast, King Saul asked his son where David was. Jonathan made excuses for his friend but Saul burst into a furious rage.

'What kind of son are you to side with my enemy? I know you are protecting him! Now go! Bring David here so I can kill him!'

Jonathan went out into the field and fired some arrows. He sent a boy to fetch them, giving the agreed sign. Then David knew his life was still in danger. Jonathan was warning him to run away.

123 DAVID, THE OUTLAW

David could think of only one place in which to hide from King Saul. He went to the priests who lived at Nob.

'I'm here on a secret mission from the king,' David said. 'I left in a hurry and have no weapon. I need something to eat, and a sword or spear, if you have one.'

Ahimelech the priest only had the special holy bread but he gave this to David to eat. The only weapon there was Goliath's sword. David took the sword away.

David moved on, but Saul's head shepherd, Doeg, was there that day. He went to tell Saul the way David had gone. He also told Saul that the priest had helped David.

'I will have all the priests killed for their part in David's escape,' Saul said in his anger.

Saul's own men would not hurt the priests, but Doeg went and killed not only Ahimelech and the other priests but everyone who lived in the town of Nob. Only one man escaped. He was Abiathar, Ahimelech's son.

Abiathar fled and found David and the men he had gathered around him. David was angry when he heard what Saul had done, and very sad for all the lost lives.

'This is all my fault,' he told Abiathar. 'You must stay here and I will keep you safe.'

124 DAVID SPARES SAUL'S LIFE

David and his men kept moving to escape from King Saul. When the Philistines attacked the town of Keilah, God told David to go and help protect the people.

So David and his men fought and defeated the Philistines and saved the people of Keilah. Saul heard of the victory and came looking for David with 3000 men.

David was camping in the hills of En Gedi when Saul came searching for him. Saul entered the entrance to the cave where David's men were hiding but he did not realise that they were there deep inside the dark cave.

'Look,' one of his men whispered to David. 'God has given you this opportunity to kill your enemy!'

David crept up to Saul and cut off a part of his cloak without him knowing. He would not kill the man God had made king. He waited until Saul had left the cave.

'King Saul!' David called. 'Look here at the cloth cut from your cloak. Now do you believe that I don't want to kill you?'

Saul wept at the sound of David's voice.

'You have been good to me today. God has blessed you. Promise that you will not kill my family when you are king.'

David promised, but he continued to hide from Saul.

125 ABIGAIL'S WISDOM

David and his men were still living rough in the hills, hiding from King Saul. For some time they had protected the shepherds of a rich but foolish man called Nabal. As the time for sheep-shearing and feasting came near, David sent some of his men to ask if any food could be spared for them.

Nabal was a man of few manners and he saw no reason to be kind to David and his men. He sent the men away rudely and with nothing.

David was angry. He told his men to arm themselves to fight.

Meanwhile a servant went to tell Nabal's wife, Abigail, how rude and unkind her husband had been. Abigail was beautiful and she was also wise. She knew what danger Nabal had placed them all in.

Abigail prepared a feast for David's men—bread and wine, roasted sheep and plenty of grain, cakes of raisins and pressed figs—and, without telling her husband, went out on a donkey into the mountains to meet David.

'Please forgive my husband's bad manners,' she asked David. 'Don't be angry with us, but accept these gifts of food. We know that God has blessed you and protects you from your enemies. Now please, shed no blood in anger.'

David accepted her gift and praised God for preventing him from killing the men there.

'Thank you,' he said to Abigail. 'Go home in safety.'

David did not forget what Abigail had done to help him. When he heard that Nabal had died, he asked her to be his wife.

126 DAVID'S NIGHT RAID

Again King Saul took his 3000 men to search for David.

David's spies watched while Saul and his army made camp. The king was surrounded by his troops and Abner, the commander of Saul's army, was by his side.

'Who will come with me to see Saul?' David asked his friends.

'I will,' offered Abishai.

When it was dark, the two men crept down to Saul's camp, where everyone was sleeping deeply. Close to King Saul's head lay his spear, its point stuck in the ground; by his side was a water jug.

'Let me kill Saul while we have the chance,' whispered Abishai to David. 'God has given his life to us.'

'No!' ordered David. 'He is still God's chosen king.'

Instead David told Abishai to pick up the spear and water jug, and they left the camp as quietly as they had come.

'Speak to me, Abner!' shouted David, from a safe distance. 'You haven't been protecting your king! Where is your master's spear and water jug?'

Saul recognised David's voice and realised what had happened. He knew that once more David had spared his life.

'May God bless you for not killing me,' cried the king.

127 SAUL'S FINAL DEFEAT

David knew that King Saul would soon be searching for him again.

He took 600 of his men and escaped to the land of the Philistines. The Philistine King Achish knew that Saul and David were enemies. He let David settle in his land. Achish preferred to have David as a friend rather than as an enemy.

Meanwhile Saul prepared to lead the Israelite army. Samuel had died and so Saul disguised himself and went to see a woman who claimed to be able to speak to the dead.

'I must talk to Samuel,' he told her.

'Surely you know that King Saul has forbidden anyone to talk to the dead! It is against God's law,' she said.

Saul reassured her that she would be safe and she called to Samuel. As soon as she saw the dead prophet, she knew that the man in front of her was King Saul himself.

'Tell me what Samuel says,' Saul commanded. 'You need to fear nothing from me.'

'Why do you call me?' asked Samuel. 'You have done all those things God told you not to do. God has left you. Tomorrow, you will be defeated by the Philistines. You and your sons will all die.'

King Achish gathered his army to fight the Israelites. He had told David that he must fight against his own people, but the Philistine commanders did not want David fighting on their side.

So when the Philistines defeated the Israelites the next day, David was not there to watch his friend Jonathan be killed in battle, or to see King Saul fall on his own sword rather than be killed by the Philistines. Israel's first king was dead.

128 DAVID, KING OF JUDAH

After Saul's death, David wanted to return to his own land.

'Shall I go back to Judah?' David asked God.

'Yes,' said God. 'Go to the town of Hebron.'

So David took his two wives and the men who had fought with him with their families and they all settled in Hebron. Men from the southern tribe of Judah came to Hebron and welcomed David and made him their king.

Meanwhile Abner, the commander of Saul's army, had made Saul's son, Ish-Bosheth, king over the northern part of the land. They did not accept David as their king. So the land was divided: Israel included the tribes in the north and Judah those in the south.

129 THE WARRING COMMANDERS

David's army, under the command of Joab, sat on one side of the pool of Gibeon. Ish-Bosheth's army, under Abner's command, was on the other side.

'Let's choose twelve champions and let them fight!' said Abner. 'Whichever side does best will win the battle.'

There was a keen contest between the two sides but all of the soldiers died; there was no winner. Then war broke out with both armies fighting each other. David's men were stronger, and Ish-Bosheth's army was defeated.

Abner fled from the battle, followed by Asahel, Joab's brother.

Abner turned and tried to reason with Asahel.

'Stop pursuing me!' shouted Abner. 'I don't want to kill you.'

Asahel would not give up, and Abner killed him with a spear.

Abner then tried to agree a truce with Joab. At sunset, he and his men called to Joab from the hilltop.

'We should be on the same side,' Abner said. 'This fighting is senseless. Let's stop now!'

So Joab agreed to end the battle, but he did not forget that Abner had killed his brother.

130 ABNER CHANGES SIDES

Over time David married more wives and had six children; each child had a different mother.

The trouble between the lands of Judah and Israel continued but David's side was stronger. Soon Abner decided to go over to David's side because King Ish-Bosheth made him very angry.

When Joab discovered that King David had made peace with Abner, he was furious. Joab found an opportunity to be alone with Abner and then he murdered him to avenge his brother's death.

David was very sad when he heard how Abner had died. He knew that he had been a brave soldier, and he mourned him openly, so all the people knew that he had not been involved in Abner's death.

131 THE MURDER OF ISH-BOSHETH

When Ish-Bosheth heard that Abner was dead, he was afraid. The whole of Israel was afraid.

Then one day, while Ish-Bosheth was taking his rest in the heat of the afternoon, two strangers arrived. They crept into the house and found the king lying on his bed. They stabbed and killed him, then cut off his head. Thinking that this would please King David, they took his head as a trophy and brought it to Hebron.

'We have brought you the head of your enemy,' they told David.

David could not believe what they had done.

'You have murdered an innocent man while he slept in his own bed!' he cried. 'You must die for your crime.'

The two men were taken out and executed, and David made sure that Ish-Bosheth's head was buried with Abner.

132 THE CAPTURE OF JERUSALEM

Once people realised that Ish-Bosheth was dead, they met together at Hebron.

'Years ago we were one nation, and we fought together against our enemies,' they said to David. 'God promised that you would look after us as a shepherd looks after his sheep. We want you to be our king now.'

So when David was 30 years old, he was made king of all Israel.

David gathered together an army and marched towards the fortified city of Jerusalem, which was set on a hill. The city was occupied by the Jebusites, a Canaanite tribe.

'You are no match for us here!' they boasted. 'Not even David will be able to defeat us.'

David found the tunnel which had been dug under the city to bring in water from the Gihon spring.

He surprised the Jebusites by entering the city through the water tunnel and was able to capture Jerusalem.

David made the fortress his capital, and from then on it became known as the City of David.

133 DAVID DANCES

Now that he was king and living in
Jerusalem, David wanted to bring the ark
of the covenant there, as a sign of God's
presence. So the ark was placed on a new
cart, and carefully guided along the road.

Suddenly one of the oxen pulling the cart stumbled. Uzzah put out
his hand and touched the ark to stop it from falling. At that moment he
fell down, dead.

'I can't bring the ark back to Jerusalem now,' said David. 'The day is
spoiled.'

So David left the ark in Obed-Edom's house.

Three months later, David was told how much God had blessed
Obed-Edom because he was looking after the ark of the covenant.
Then David knew he had to bring the ark back to Jerusalem so that God
would bless the whole nation.

Everyone gathered as the ark was carried into Jerusalem. They sang
to God and David celebrated by joining the people and dancing before
God.

Michal, David's wife, saw him dancing in the streets.

'What a fool he is making of himself!' she thought.

When the celebrations were over, Michal went out to meet David.

'I saw you today, dancing with the people!' she sneered. 'You didn't
behave the way a king should.'

'It doesn't matter what you think of me,' said David to his wife. 'I was
praising God and dancing for God. And he chose me to be king rather
than your father, Saul.'

134 GOD'S DWELLING PLACE

David built a palace made of cedar wood in Jerusalem. His enemies knew that God was with him and Israel enjoyed a time of peace.

One day David spoke to Nathan, the prophet, about the ark of the covenant.

'It does not seem right that I live here in a palace while the ark lives in a tent,' said David. 'I think I should build a temple fit for God.'

That night Nathan heard God speaking to him.

'I don't want David to build a temple for me,' said God. 'I have been happy to move from place to place with my people. My plan for David is to make Israel into a great nation. I will make him a great king and I will never stop loving him. After David will come one of his sons. I will also love him, and he can build me a temple. David's family will be kings for a long time to come.'

Nathan told David everything that God had said. David was amazed at the plans God had for him, and he was humbled.

'I don't know why you have chosen me or looked after me,' said David, 'or why you have told me your plans. I do know that you are a great God, and you always keep your promises.'

135 THE GOD WHO KNOWS EVERYTHING

David wrote this song as a prayer to God.

'You have looked deep into my heart, Lord, and you know all about me. You know when I am resting and when I am working, and from heaven you see my thoughts.

'You notice everything I do and everywhere I go. Before I even speak a word you know what I will say, and you protect me from every side.

'I can't understand this! Is there anywhere I could hide from you? If I were to climb to the heavens, you would be there. If I were to dig down to the world of the dead, you would also be there.

'If I had wings and flew across the ocean, even then your powerful arm would guide and protect me. If I hid in the dark you would see me because day and night are all the same to you.

'You are the one who put me together inside my mother's body, and I praise you because of the wonderful way you created me. Everything you do is marvellous!

'Nothing about me is hidden from you! I was secretly woven together deep in the earth below, but you saw my body being formed. Even before I was born, you had written in your book everything I would do.

'Your thoughts are far beyond my understanding, much more than I could ever imagine. I try to count your thoughts, but they outnumber the grains of sand on the beach. And when I awake, I will find you nearby.

'Look deep into my heart, God, and discover everything about me. Don't let me follow evil ways, but teach me to do all that is honest and good.'

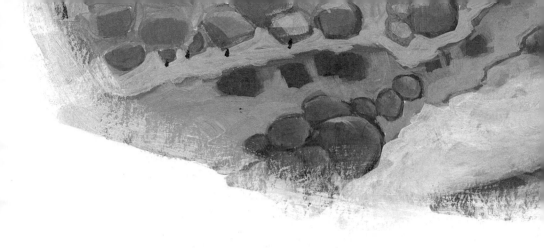

136 DAVID'S KINDNESS

David often thought of his friend Jonathan, who had died in battle.

'Does Saul have any family still living?' David asked one day. 'I would like to be kind to one of his relatives for Jonathan's sake.'

'There is one called Mephibosheth,' Ziba told the king. 'He is Jonathan's son. He was dropped when he was five years old and both his feet are damaged.'

'I'd like to help him,' said David. 'Bring him here.'

Mephibosheth was anxious about being brought before King David.

'There is no need to be afraid, Mephibosheth,' David told him. 'Your father was my greatest friend. I promised to look after his family. Come and live in the palace with me and I will give you the land that belonged to your family.'

Mephibosheth was amazed that a great king like David should keep his promise and take care of him. He lived in Jerusalem and was treated as part of David's family from that time on.

137 DAVID BREAKS GOD'S RULES

One evening in springtime, when the Israelite army was away fighting, King David went out on to the palace rooftop.

As he looked across the city, he saw a woman bathing in the courtyard of a nearby house. She did not know she was being watched. She was a very beautiful woman.

David called a servant and asked who she was.

'That's Bathsheba,' the servant replied, 'Uriah's wife.'

David knew Uriah. He was a soldier in his army. At that moment, David did not care whose wife she was. He wanted Bathsheba for himself.

'Bring Bathsheba here,' he ordered.

Bathsheba came to the palace, and David made love to her.

Some time later, Bathsheba sent a message to David.

'I'm pregnant,' she said. 'The baby I am carrying is yours.'

138 URIAH DIES IN BATTLE

David was anxious about Bathsheba's news. He quickly thought of a plan to cover up the wrong he had done. David sent a message to Joab at the battlefront, asking him to send Uriah home.

Uriah returned to Jerusalem and David asked him about the progress of the war with the Ammonites. Afterwards David told him to go home, relax and spend time with his wife, but Uriah would not go home.

'How can I enjoy myself while all my fellow soldiers are fighting?' he said. 'It would be wrong.'

Sadly, David let Uriah return to the battlefield. He asked him to take with him a letter for Joab.

'Make sure Uriah fights on the front line,' the letter said. 'Leave him undefended so that he will die.'

Joab had besieged the city. He let Uriah fight close to the city walls so that he was killed by an arrow.

When a messenger came with the news that Uriah was dead, David felt relieved. Now he could hide what he had done wrong. Bathsheba mourned her husband's death. Then David brought her to the palace and she became his wife.

Time passed and Bathsheba gave birth to a baby boy. God knew all that had happened, from David's deceit through to his arranging of Uriah's death. God was angry with David.

139 NATHAN'S MESSAGE

God sent the prophet Nathan to David with a message.

'There were once two men,' said Nathan. 'One of them was a wealthy farmer with many sheep and cattle. The other man was poor with just one little lamb. She was very special to him.

'One day a guest came to stay with the rich man. Instead of killing one of his own sheep, he stole the lamb from the poor man and cooked it.'

'That's terrible!' David said. 'He must be punished!'

'You are the rich man,' said Nathan. 'God has given you so much. He made you king over his people and saved you from Saul's anger. He gave you wives and children, yet you took another man's wife and made sure that her husband died. God is angry.'

Then David put his head in his hands. He knew that everything Nathan had said was true.

'I am so sorry,' said David. 'I have sinned against God.'

'God forgives you,' said Nathan. 'But there will still be consequences of the wrong that you have done.'

Not long after this, Bathsheba's son became very ill and although for a whole week David did nothing except pray to God for his life, the little boy died. David comforted Bathsheba as best he could.

In time, she had another little boy. They named him Solomon.

140 DAVID'S SORROW

David prayed to God after Nathan had come to him.

'Have mercy on me, dear God, because of your great and constant love. Wash away my sin and let me feel your forgiveness.

'I know that what I have done is wrong; I cannot forget how terrible it is and I am so sorry.

'I know, too, that you are holy and it is you that I have wronged; I have betrayed your trust and let you down.

'Wash away my sin, dear God; take away my guilt.

'Forgive me and do not hold this wrong against me for ever.

'I know you don't want empty sacrifices or outward signs of my guilt; you want only to know that I am really sorry and that I will not sin in this way again.

'Make my heart pure, and help me to do only what is right.

'Give me back the joy I have in loving and serving you so that others may know and love you too.'

141 DAVID IS BETRAYED

David had many sons, but because they had different mothers, they were often jealous of each other. Amnon, David's eldest son, fell in love with his half-sister, Tamar. When Tamar's brother, Absalom, found out that he had forced her to sleep with him, he was angry and arranged for him to be killed.

When David heard what had happened to his eldest son, he was grief-stricken. Absalom fled the country and stayed away from his father. But David loved his sons. He missed Amnon because he was dead; he also missed Absalom. Joab saw how sad David was. After some years had passed, he persuaded David to let Absalom come home.

Absalom was popular with the people. He dreamed of being king one day and gathered a band of men around him. Before long a messenger came to David in Jerusalem.

'Absalom has been proclaimed king in Hebron,' he announced.

'Then we must go quickly!' said David. 'Absalom will kill us all.'

David and his friends fled from Jerusalem. When he found that Ahithophel had also joined Absalom, David wept. He had been betrayed by his son and by his trusted adviser.

'Oh, God,' prayed David. 'Please make Ahithophel give Absalom bad advice.'

Then David told Hushai to return to Jerusalem and pretend to join Absalom.

142 HUSHAI TRICKS ABSALOM

When Absalom arrived in Jerusalem, Hushai came to meet him.

'Long live the king!' said Hushai.

Absalom was suspicious.

'Why are you here?' he asked. 'Is this how you serve your friend, my father David?'

'I will serve the man God and all the people have chosen as king,' Hushai replied.

Absalom then turned to Ahithophel and asked him what he should do next.

'Let me choose 12,000 men to attack David tonight,' said Ahithophel. 'He and his men will be tired and anxious. It will be easy to kill David, and then I will lead his troops back to Jerusalem, and there will be peace.'

It was a good plan, but Absalom was undecided.

'What do you think?' he asked Hushai.

Hushai thought quickly. 'Ahithophel has not given you good advice,' he said. 'David will know you will try to come after him. He will hide away from his men. Wait and then lead the army yourself.'

Absalom liked Hushai's plan. Secretly, Hushai warned David.

143 THE DEATH OF ABSALOM

David divided his men into three groups and planned to go with them to fight.

'You must stay here,' they told him. 'If anything happens to you, everything is lost. You can send us help if we need it.'

'Do what you have to do,' David told them, 'but please do not harm Absalom!'

The two armies engaged in battle in the forest. David's soldiers defeated Absalom's men and thousands of men died. Then Absalom came riding through the forest, his hair flowing behind him. Suddenly, it was caught in the branches of an oak tree and he was pulled from his mule and left dangling in mid-air.

'I saw Absalom hanging from a tree,' said one of the soldiers to Joab.

'What? Why didn't you kill him?' asked Joab.

'King David gave instructions that we shouldn't hurt his son,' the man said. 'I wouldn't dare disobey such an order.'

Joab and his armour-bearers found Absalom and killed him.

Two men ran with the news of their victory to David. Joab warned them not to say that Absalom was dead.

'The victory is ours!' cried Ahimaaz who got there first.

'Is Absalom alive?' David.

'I wish all your enemies would end up like him,' the messenger replied.

Then David wept for his son.

'Oh, my dear son, Absalom,' cried David. 'How I wish I could have died instead of you!'

144 DAVID KEEPS HIS PROMISE

King David grew old and unwell and soon the affairs of the nation were of less importance to him. David's fourth son, Adonijah, decided to take over from his father and rule the people. Joab supported him but Zadok, Benaiah and Nathan, the prophet, remained loyal to David.

Nathan went to see Bathsheba.

'Have you heard that Adonijah has made himself king?' Nathan asked her. 'You had better warn King David. Didn't he promise you that Solomon would be king after him?'

Bathsheba went to see King David.

'Solomon will be king,' David assured Bathsheba. 'Let Solomon go to Gihon, riding on my mule so that he can be anointed.'

Zadok took the horn of oil and anointed him king.

'Long live King Solomon!' shouted the people.

Adonijah had been feasting with his friends and supporters. They heard the sound of music and celebration.

'David has made Solomon king!' a messenger announced. 'Zadok has anointed him.'

Adonijah's supporters realised they might now be in danger. They made their way to their own homes while Adonijah fled to the temple.

145 DAVID'S LAST DAYS

When David knew that he was dying, he sent for Solomon.

'I am soon to die and go the way that all of us must. The throne of Israel will belong to you and to your descendants. Remember to obey God and to follow all the laws that Moses left us. If you do as God says, he will bless you in everything you do.'

'Watch Joab,' warned David. 'Remember that he is a murderer. Make sure that he is punished.'

Solomon listened carefully to his father. Not long afterwards, David died and was buried in Jerusalem. He had ruled for 40 years, and under his leadership Israel had become a strong nation.

146 ADONIJAH'S REQUEST

Solomon sat on David's throne and ruled as king. Adonijah still hoped to take some power for himself.

Adonijah went to Bathsheba with a request.

'Solomon will listen to you,' he said. 'Please ask if I may marry Abishag now that our father is dead.'

Bathsheba told Solomon what Adonijah had asked for, but Solomon knew he wanted much more.

'Adonijah cannot be trusted,' Solomon told his mother. 'We will not be safe until he is dead.'

Solomon sent Benaiah to execute Adonijah, and when he was dead, Joab ran away and hid, knowing that he was in danger for supporting him. Solomon had also given orders for Joab's execution for the murders he had committed.

Benaiah found Joab and killed him too.

Then Solomon promoted Benaiah so that he was commander of the army in Joab's place. He also made Zadok the priest.

Solomon was now properly in control of Israel.

147 GOD'S GIFT TO SOLOMON

Solomon loved God and followed his father's advice by keeping all God's commandments.

One night, after a day of worshipping God at Gibeon, Solomon had a strange dream in which God appeared to him.

'Ask for anything you want,' God said, 'and I will give it to you.'

Solomon replied, 'You blessed my father David, and you gave him a son who would rule after him. You have already been so good to me, allowing me to be king in his place. I know nothing; I am young and inexperienced. What I want most of all is the ability to make wise judgements so that I can rule the people fairly.'

God was pleased with Solomon's answer.

'You have asked for wisdom,' said God, 'when you could have chosen wealth, or revenge over your enemies, or a long life. I will give you what you have asked for, so that everyone will be amazed, and you will always be remembered for your wisdom, but I will also give you wealth and power. And if you obey me, I will give you long life too.'

When Solomon woke up, he clearly remembered his dream and all that God had promised him.

148 SOLOMON'S WISDOM

One day, two women came to see Solomon.

'Your majesty,' cried one of the women. 'This woman and I live in the same house. I gave birth to a baby son while she was in the house with me. Then three days later, she also had a baby son.

'We both went to sleep with our babies cuddled up next to us. This woman rolled on her baby while she was sleeping and he died. She came to me while I slept and swapped her dead baby for my living son. When I awoke, I knew that the dead baby was not mine.'

'That's not true!' shouted the other woman. 'My son is alive; yours is dead!'

'Bring me a sword!' ordered Solomon. 'Divide the baby into two parts so that each woman can have a share!' Solomon knew that the real mother would not let her child die in this way.

'Don't harm him!' the first woman pleaded with the king. 'Let her have the baby.'

'No, what the king says is fair!' replied the other woman.

Immediately Solomon knew which woman was the baby's mother.

'Give the first woman her baby,' Solomon ordered. 'She is his mother.'

Everyone in Israel was amazed. They knew that God had given him wisdom to judge between them fairly.

Solomon wrote down many of his wise sayings:

'Listen to what your parents tell you. Their teaching will build a good character in the same way as good clothes make you look smart.

'A wise child pays attention when parents correct him, but a foolish one never admits that he is wrong.

'If you love your children, you will correct them when they are naughty.

'The start of an argument is like a hole in a dam. Stop it quickly before it gets out of control.

'There is nothing but sadness and sorrow for a parent whose child does foolish things.

'Discipline your children while they are young enough to learn. If you don't, you are helping them to destroy themselves.

'Children are blessed if their father is honest and does what is right.

'Anyone who thinks it isn't wrong to steal from his parents is no better than a common thief.'

150 WISDOM ABOUT FRIENDS

'A gentle answer can turn anger away, but a fierce reply can make things worse.

'Gossip is spread by wicked people; they stir up trouble and break up friendships.

'It is better to eat bread and water with your friends than to eat a feast with your enemies.

'If you want people to like you, forgive them when they do something wrong. Remembering wrongs can break up a friendship.

'If you want to stay out of trouble, be careful about what you say.

'Don't make friends with people who have hot tempers. You might learn their habits and find it hard to change.

'A friend means well, even if he hurts you. If an enemy starts pretending to be your friend, trouble is bound to follow.'

151 WISDOM FOR LIFE

'Trust in the Lord with all your heart. Don't rely on what you think you know. Ask for God's help in all you do and he will guide you.

'Do good to those who are in need whenever you can. Don't tell someone you will help them tomorrow if you can help them today.

'Be careful how you think; your life is shaped by your thoughts. Speak only the truth; have nothing to do with lies.

'Be generous, and you will do well. Help others and you will be helped.

'Wise people are careful to stay out of trouble, but foolish people act without thinking.

'If you want to be happy, be kind to the poor. Never despise or belittle other people.

'If you oppress poor people, you insult God who made them; kindness to the poor is an act of worship.

'Do what is right and fair; that pleases God more than any gift you can offer him.

'Sensible people will see trouble coming and avoid it, but a foolish person will walk into trouble and regret it later.

'Don't wear yourself out trying to get rich. Your money can disappear in a flash as if it had grown wings and flown away.

'You will never succeed in life if you try to hide your sins. Confess them and God will show mercy and forgive you.

'It is better to have no money and be honest than to be rich and dishonest.'

152 A TEMPLE FOR GOD

While Solomon was king, there was peace in Israel. The time was right for Solomon to build a temple for God.

King Hiram of Tyre had been a friend of King David. When he sent ambassadors to David's son, Solomon, he sent back a message.

'God told my father David that a temple would be built after his reign when there was peace in the land. Now that time has come. I want you to fell the best cedar trees in Lebanon so I can start building. I will pay you whatever you ask.'

The king of Tyre was happy to make an agreement and he supplied Solomon with all the wood he needed, making rafts out of the logs of cedar and pine and floating them down the coast.

God told Solomon how the temple should be designed and constructed. The stones were prepared in the quarry and brought to the chosen site. Solomon lined the internal walls with carved wood and covered them with gold. He filled the temple with all the things that God wanted, taken from the tent of meeting.

Finally, in front of all Israel's elders, the ark of the covenant, which contained the stone tablets bearing God's laws, was brought to the temple and put into the Holy of Holies. The cloud of God's presence filled the temple so that the priests were dazzled by the light.

Then Solomon asked God's blessing on the people.

153 SOLOMON'S PRAYER

'Lord God of Israel, you are like no one else,' prayed Solomon. 'No one in heaven above, no one beneath the earth shows such love and compassion; no one else keeps promises as you do.

'Lord, I have built you a house, but I know that even heaven cannot contain you, for you are a great God! Let this temple be a place where your people can come when we need your help. Whether we bow before the altar here, or whether we bow in its direction when we are far away, hear our prayers.

'We will come when we fear our enemies; we will come when there is drought or famine; we will come when we have sinned—for there is no man, woman or child who does not sin and break your laws—and we will ask your forgiveness. Then, Lord, hear us from heaven and have mercy on us. Keep the promises that you made to Moses and our ancestors, that we will be your people, and that you will be our God.'

Then Solomon turned to the people and prayed again.

'We ask that God will be with us and bless us and help us to keep his laws, so that all the peoples on earth will know that the Lord is God, and that there is no other.'

God appeared to Solomon some time after this and spoke to him.

'I have heard your prayers, and I will bless you and this house that you have made for me. But,' God warned Solomon, 'if you disobey me and neglect to follow my laws, your children will not be kings, and this house will become a ruin. People will pass by and know that it is because you did not obey my laws and because you did not love the God who brought you out of Egypt.'

154 THE VISIT OF THE QUEEN OF SHEBA

Reports about Solomon's wealth and wisdom were carried through the traders who passed through his land. Far away, the queen of Sheba heard stories of Solomon's greatness. She rode across the deserts of Arabia and along the Red Sea coast on a four-poster bed covered in cushions, with a roof to protect her from the sun.

Her arrival in Jerusalem was greeted with great interest. The queen had brought with her gifts for King Solomon: gold and precious stones, exotic spices and items of furniture.

The queen saw the palace that Solomon had built with lavish crimson and purple curtains; she walked in his vineyards and gardens; she saw his many fine horses and chariots; she tasted good food and wine. She listened to singers with exotic musical instruments.

She watched Solomon worship God in the temple and found that he could answer questions about so many things; his wisdom was inexhaustible.

'I heard all about you in my country,' the queen said to Solomon, 'but I couldn't believe it was true. Now I know that you are even greater than your reputation. Let me praise your God for making you such a great and wise king!'

155 SOLOMON'S POWER AND WEALTH

Solomon planted olive, spice and nut trees and studied the ways of spiders, locusts and harvesting ants. He knew about plants and animals, birds, reptiles and fish.

As Solomon's reputation grew, he became richer and richer. Many visitors came to consult him and ask for his help; each one brought expensive gifts. He traded with many different nations, and his fleet of ships brought him back gold and silver, ivory, apes and peacocks.

Soon Solomon had so much gold that everything in his palace was made of it; silver was worthless because there was so much gold. Solomon's throne was made out of ivory, with golden armrests and golden embroidery and a calf's head carved on the back of it. On either side of the throne was a huge golden lion. Six steps led up to the throne and on each side of each step was another golden lion. No one had ever seen anything so spectacular before.

Solomon had a weakness. He married foreign wives, who bowed down to idols and did not know the one true God. He had forgotten God's warnings.

156 THE BROKEN PROMISE

As the years passed, Solomon not only loved his many wives, he also began to worship their gods.

God was angry with Solomon.

'I warned you not to worship these idols as the other nations do. You have broken your promise to me,' said God. 'I will not take the kingdom from you yet, because I made a promise to your father, David, but I will take the kingdom from your son.'

A young man called Jeroboam worked very hard for Solomon. One day as Jeroboam was walking on the road outside Jerusalem, the prophet Ahijah came to him. Ahijah took off the new cloak he was wearing and ripped it into twelve pieces.

'Take them!' he said, giving ten pieces to Jeroboam. 'This is a picture of what God will do for you. Once Solomon is dead, God will make you king over ten of the tribes of Israel. Remember to follow God's commandments and serve him well.'

Solomon heard what had happened and tried to kill Jeroboam, but Jeroboam escaped to Egypt and hid there.

157 THE DIVIDED KINGDOM

When Solomon died, Jeroboam left Egypt and joined with the people from the northern tribes of Israel at Shechem.

Solomon's son, Rehoboam, also went to Shechem, hoping that the people would proclaim him king. Instead, they challenged him.

'Your father, King Solomon, made us work hard. If you want us to make you king now, you must promise to make our work easier.'

Rehoboam told the people to return in three days, and meanwhile he consulted his father's old officials.

'You have no choice,' they advised him.

Rehoboam did not like their answer so he asked his friends instead. They told him not to give in but to warn the people of what would happen if they did not obey him!

So Rehoboam gave them the answer his friends had suggested. It was not the right answer!

'You are not one of us; you are not our king! We will not serve you or work for you.'

Rehoboam had made his first mistake. He returned to Jerusalem where only the tribe of Judah followed him. The ten northern tribes of Israel made Jeroboam their king.

The kingdom of Israel was divided. Now there was no longer one nation but two.

158 KING JEROBOAM'S DISOBEDIENCE

Jeroboam had built two cities at Shechem and Penuel but the temple was in Jerusalem under Rehoboam's control. If he let the people return to worship God, they might decide to follow King Rehoboam instead. He couldn't let that happen.

Jeroboam made two golden calves and told the people to worship them instead of going into Jerusalem. He even went to worship the golden calves himself. He made priests out of the people instead of the Levites, and he introduced new feast days.

'Be warned!' shouted a prophet from Judah. 'God has seen these things you have done and chosen Josiah, one of King David's descendants, to overthrow you. God will make your altar crumble and the ashes of the sacrifice will fall on the ground.'

'Seize him!' Jeroboam said, pointing at the prophet. At that moment Jeroboam's hand was paralysed. He could not move it.

Jeroboam watched helplessly as the altar cracked and crumbled before his eyes, scattering the ashes over the ground.

'Ask God to help me!' he begged. 'Give me back the use of my hand.'

The prophet prayed for Jeroboam and his hand was restored. Jeroboam soon forgot the prophet's warning. He continued to disobey God.

159 A TERRIBLE WARNING

Jeroboam's son, Abijah, became ill. It became clear that he might die.

'Go to Ahijah, the prophet in Shiloh,' Jeroboam told his wife. 'Ask him what will happen to our son. But disguise yourself; don't let him know that you are the king's wife.'

Jeroboam's wife took some bread, cakes and honey as gifts for the prophet, and went to Shiloh.

Ahijah's sight was failing for he was an old man, but God told him that Jeroboam's wife was coming, and that she would be disguised. God gave Ahijah a message for her.

'I know who you are, wife of Jeroboam,' said Ahijah. 'I have bad news for you, given to me by God himself. He knows everything your husband the king has done. Your family will be punished because of his sins. Terrible things will happen! God has seen that your child is good. God will take him now so that he will be spared a worse fate. When you get home, your son will die, and his death will sadden everyone.'

Jeroboam's wife returned home to find that her son had died.

160 WAR AND DEFEAT

The kingdom of Judah was strengthening at this time. Rehoboam fortified his cities against attack and gave each of his sons a city to rule over.

Rehoboam also built many shrines and altars to other gods and his people followed him. He did all those things that his ancestors had done which had made God angry. He did not follow God's commandments or love him as his grandfather, David, had done.

God allowed Shishak, the king of Egypt, to attack Jerusalem. Shishak plundered the temple and the palace, removing the golden treasures that Solomon had made.

Israel and Judah fought each other. Peace between the nations was over.

161 THE WICKED KING AHAB

Kings came and went in Israel. Nadab, Jeroboam's son, was overthrown by Baasha; Elah, Baasha's son, was overthrown by Zimri; Omri overthrew Zimri. Each king was worse than the one before. Not one of them served God as King David had. All God's commandments were broken again and again.

When Omri's son Ahab became king, the evil in the land was greater than it had ever been. Ahab married a woman called Jezebel, daughter of the king of Sidon, who worshipped the fertility god, Baal.

Ahab openly worshipped Baal too and made a temple for his statue.

The people who had once worshipped God as creator of all the world now bowed down to idols they had made with their own hands.

162 ELIJAH BRINGS BAD NEWS

In the mountains of Gilead, there lived a man called Elijah.

Elijah was a prophet. He heard God speak and, unlike so many of the people of Israel at that time, he tried to follow God's ways.

God chose Elijah to go to see King Ahab.

'God, the one true God, has sent me here,' said Elijah. 'There will be no rain, not even any early morning dew, for some years. There will be a drought until God chooses to send rain again.'

The king was angry at the news, but Elijah did not stay to see what he would do.

'Leave this place now and go eastwards,' God told Elijah. 'You will find all you need at the Cherith Brook.'

Elijah found the brook on the eastern side of the River Jordan. He made himself a shelter there and drank the water from the brook. God sent ravens with food for him to eat, and Elijah had everything that he needed.

It did not rain. Day after day, the hot sun beat down and the dawn brought no dew. The ground became dry and parched. After a while, the water in the brook dried up.

163 THE OIL THAT DIDN'T RUN OUT

God had already provided for Elijah's needs.

'Go to Zarephath,' God told Elijah. 'There is a woman there who will provide you with food.'

Elijah travelled to Sidon and when he reached the city gates of the place called Zarephath, he saw a woman gathering sticks for firewood.

'Some water, please,' Elijah asked her. 'And a little bread to eat?'

'I have no bread baked,' she replied, 'for the drought has made us all hungry. I have just a little flour and oil left, and I am here gathering these few sticks to make a fire. I will cook the last meal for myself and my only son. Then we must die, for there is no more.'

'Don't be afraid,' said Elijah. 'Go and bake this bread as you were planning to do. Only share a little of it with me. God will bless you. Your flour and oil will not run out until God sends rain again.'

The woman went home and baked the bread. She shared it with Elijah and her son, and there was still enough flour and oil for another meal.

Again the woman used the flour and oil so they could share their last meal. Again there was just enough left.

Many days passed and God made sure that the woman and her son and Elijah had enough to eat.

164 ELIJAH SAVES
A LITTLE BOY

Elijah stayed in a room in the woman's house.

After some time had passed, the woman's son grew ill. She sat by his bedside, watching, holding him in her arms until he drew his last breath and died.

The woman was overcome by grief and anger.

'Why did you come here?' she sobbed. 'What have I done to you that my son should die like this?'

Elijah took the dead boy in his arms and carried him upstairs to his own room. He laid the boy on his bed and prayed.

'Lord God,' he cried, 'why have you allowed this to happen to the woman whose home I have shared? Please give the boy back his life!'

God heard Elijah's prayer. Suddenly, the boy started to breathe again. Elijah lifted him gently and carried him back to his mother.

'Look! Your son is alive!' Elijah said.

The woman hugged her son and smiled at Elijah, the tears still in her eyes.

'Now I know you are God's friend,' she said.

165
THE THIRD
YEAR OF
DROUGHT

It had not rained for nearly three years. King Ahab sent the prophet Obadiah to search for any green place left in the land where food might be found for the animals. If none could be found, the animals would have to be slaughtered.

Before long, Obadiah met Elijah. Elijah asked him to bring the king to him for he had a message from God.

'My lord,' said Obadiah, 'King Ahab has had people searching the whole country for you. I cannot go before him and tell him I have found you now. You are sure to disappear again, and he will kill me!'

Elijah promised he would stay to meet King Ahab.

Obadiah brought King Ahab, who was very angry.

'You are a troublemaker!' he shouted at Elijah.

'You are the one who has brought trouble to the land,' said Elijah, 'because you stopped worshipping God and started to worship false idols. Now we will settle this matter. Call all the people to Mount Carmel, and bring all the false prophets who are your wife's friends.'

King Ahab sent for all the people and for all the prophets of Baal and Asherah. The word went out that there would be a contest between them and the one true God who had protected Elijah through the years of drought.

So the people came and with them the 450 prophets of Baal. They gathered on Mount Carmel.

166 THE CONTEST ON THE MOUNTAIN

Elijah stood on Mount Carmel in front of King Ahab and all the people.

'Today you must choose whom you will serve,' said Elijah. 'If the living God is the real God, then choose him and follow him. If Baal is God, then serve and follow him. It is time to make up your minds and do what is right.

'I am the only prophet here who worships the one true God,' he said, 'while there are 450 prophets here who worship Baal. We will each prepare a sacrifice. You must call upon Baal to send down fire to burn it up; I will ask my God to do the same. Then we will see which is the one true God who can send down fire.'

The prophets agreed. They prepared a bull for the sacrifice and all day they prayed to Baal to send down fire.

Nothing happened.

'Is your god asleep?' Elijah asked. 'Is he on holiday so that he can't answer?'

The prophets prayed and shouted even louder, but still there was no answer. The prophets of Baal had failed. There was no fire on the altar they had prepared. Now it was Elijah's turn.

167 THE ONE TRUE GOD

Elijah did not just make an altar as the other prophets had done. He used twelve stones to represent the twelve tribes of Israel and remind the people that they were God's people. He dug a deep trench around the altar and then prepared his sacrifice. Finally, Elijah asked for large jars to be filled with water and poured all over the wood and the sacrifice so that it ran down into the trench. Elijah's sacrifice was soaking wet; no accident could cause it to burn.

Then Elijah stepped out in front of the people and prayed. Elijah prayed that God would hear him so that the people would believe once more that he was their God too, and would worship him.

When Elijah stopped praying, God answered.

God sent down fire. God sent down fire which burned the bull, the stones and the water from the trench. The people fell on their knees and cried out, 'The Lord is God! The Lord—he is God!'

Elijah called for the false prophets to be put to death. Then he watched as black clouds began to form and the wind rose and God sent rain once more upon the land.

168 JEZEBEL'S DEATH THREATS

When Ahab told Queen Jezebel that Elijah had killed all her prophets, she was furious. She threatened to kill Elijah too. He was terrified and ran away into the desert.

Elijah found a broom tree and sat under it in the shade. He was tired and he was frightened. He felt he couldn't take any more.

'Let me die,' he said to God. 'I have had enough.' In his exhaustion, Elijah fell asleep.

After a while, an angel came and touched him.

'Get up; have something to eat,' said the angel.

Elijah looked up and saw some water and freshly baked bread. He ate the bread and drank the water. Then he fell asleep again.

The angel touched Elijah for a second time.

'Eat some more and refresh yourself for the journey ahead,' the angel said.

Elijah ate again. Then he set out for Mount Horeb, the mountain of God.

169 EARTHQUAKE, FIRE AND WHISPER

When Elijah reached Mount Horeb, he found a cave and sheltered there for the night.

'What are you doing here, Elijah?' asked God.

Elijah had been thinking about all that had happened since he had been serving God as his prophet. He had tried to encourage God's people to obey him, but still they seemed to go their own ways.

'I have done my best to serve you,' said Elijah, 'but no one listens. And now they are trying to kill me!'

God heard what was in Elijah's heart and understood that he was discouraged and frightened.

'Stand on the mountain,' said God, 'and watch me pass by.'

A powerful wind stirred and ripped through the mountains, shattering the rocks in its path, but God was not in the wind.

An earthquake cracked open the rocky ground and moved everything in its path, but God was not in the earthquake.

Then there was a fire, but God was not in the fire.

Finally, there was a gentle whisper. Elijah left the cave, and stood on the mountain with his cloak wrapped round him.

'Go back and anoint Jehu king of Israel and Elisha to succeed you. Those who have disobeyed will be punished but I will save those who still trust me.'

170 GOD'S NEW PROPHET

Elijah went to find Elisha. He was ploughing a field with a pair of oxen.

Elijah went to him, took off his cloak and flung it around Elisha's shoulders. The young man knew what this meant: he was to serve God by helping Elijah and learning from him.

Elisha left his oxen and ran after Elijah.

'Let me first go back to say goodbye to my parents and then I will come with you,' he said.

Elisha burned his ploughs, killed the oxen and cooked them. He gave the cooked meat to the people to eat. Now his past life was over. He was ready to follow Elijah and to serve God as a prophet.

171 QUEEN JEZEBEL'S PLOT

Near King Ahab's palace lived a man called Naboth who owned a vineyard.

'Your vineyard would make an ideal garden for me,' the king said to Naboth one day. 'Name your price and sell it to me or I will give you a better vineyard somewhere else.'

Naboth's vineyard had belonged to his father and his grandfather. He didn't want to sell it to anyone.

Ahab had set his heart on the vineyard. He went home, shut himself away in his room and sulked.

Queen Jezebel couldn't believe what she saw.

'What are you doing here, feeling sorry for yourself? You're the king! You can have anything you want!'

So Jezebel plotted against Naboth to get the king what he wanted. She organised for Naboth to be invited to a feast where two men would be paid to lie about him and accuse him of treason in front of all the people.

The plan worked. Naboth was taken and stoned to death.

Now there was no one to stop King Ahab taking the vineyard for himself. God sent Elijah to him with a message.

Ahab was walking around the vineyard making plans when he saw Elijah. He knew it could only mean trouble.

'Did you really think God would be happy if you killed a man to take what he owns?' said Elijah. 'You will die for what you have done to Naboth. Your queen will die for her part in this and your family will be punished.'

Ahab listened to Elijah and was sorry and afraid. God decided to give him another chance. For the next few years, there was peace in the land.

172 A WICKED KING'S DEATH

In Judah, King Jehoshaphat had become not only powerful but feared by all the nations around him. Unlike King Ahab in Israel, Jehoshaphat destroyed foreign idols and tried to follow God's ways as David had before him.

One day he went to visit King Ahab. Ahab prepared a great feast for him. He wanted Jehoshaphat's help.

'Join with me and fight against Ramoth Gilead!' Ahab asked.

'I will help you,' Jehoshaphat replied. 'What does God say? Is there a prophet here we can consult?'

King Ahab brought various prophets to Jehoshaphat, all of whom said that God would give them victory. Then Ahab said that there was one man, Micaiah, who always brought bad news. Jehoshaphat wanted to hear what he had to say.

'Go to war and you will be successful!' Micaiah said.

'Tell me exactly what God has told you,' said the king.

'God has told all your prophets to tell you to fight so that you will go to battle and die.'

Ahab was angry and had Micaiah locked up. He would fight, with or without God's help. He told Jehoshaphat to wear his royal robes into battle, but Ahab rode his chariot in disguise.

The enemy wanted only King Ahab's death. With God's help, they found him. An arrow pierced the chinks in his armour and wounded him. He watched the battle, propped up in the chariot until sunset, when, finally, King Ahab died.

173 A CHARIOT TO HEAVEN

It was time for Elijah's ministry to end. Elisha knew that he was spending his last day on earth with the prophet he had learned so much from.

Elisha walked with Elijah from Gilgal.

'Stay here while I go to Gilgal,' Elijah said to his friend.

Elisha refused. 'I will come with you,' he said.

Elijah took off his cloak, rolled it up, and struck the water with it. A pathway appeared through the river so that the two prophets could cross safely to the other side.

'Soon I must leave you. Is there anything I can do for you before I go?' asked Elijah.

'Give me twice as much of your faith and power,' said Elisha.

'This is something only God can give. If you see me leave this earth, you will have what you have asked for,' said Elijah.

Then a chariot of fire appeared in the sky and separated Elijah from Elisha. Elijah was taken up into heaven in a whirlwind.

Elisha picked up Elijah's cloak and rolled it up. He struck the River Jordan and a pathway appeared through the water.

Some prophets had been watching from a distance.

'God has given Elisha the faith and power of Elijah,' they said to each other.

174
GOD SENDS WATER IN THE DESERT

When Ahab's son Joram
became king after his father's
death, the king of Moab
refused to send him the lambs and wool which they had sent Ahab in
return for peace.

Joram joined with King Jehoshaphat and the king of Edom, and they
rode out across the desert to fight against Moab. Before long they had
run out of water for themselves and their animals.

'Is there no prophet here so that we can find out what God wants us
to do?' asked King Jehoshaphat.

'Elisha is here,' an officer answered. 'He used to help the prophet
Elijah.'

The kings went down to Elisha, but he would not speak to King Joram.

'Bring a harpist here, so that I may hear what God has to say, for
King Jehoshaphat's sake,' he said.

God told Elisha that God would send water and give them victory
over Moab.

The next morning, as God had promised, water was flowing from the
land of Edom and filled the desert. The people had plenty to drink and
to water their animals; but more than this, the people of Moab came
and saw the sun shining on the water, red as blood. It seemed to them
that the kings had killed each other in battle. They thought it would be
easy to plunder their camp. When they did so, the armies chased them
away, invaded their land and had victory over Moab, just as Elisha had
told them.

175 THE WIDOW'S DEBT

One day a woman came to ask for Elisha's help. Her husband had been a prophet, but when he died, he owed money.

'I cannot repay his creditor,' she told Elisha. 'The man wants to take my two sons away to be his slaves as payment for the debt.'

'What do you have in your home?' Elisha asked her. 'Tell me how I can help you.'

'Nothing,' replied the woman, 'except a little olive oil.'

'Go to your neighbours,' Elisha told her. 'Ask them to give you as many empty jars as they have. Collect as many as you can. Then go home to your sons, shut the door, and pour oil into all of the jars.'

The woman did as Elisha told her. She collected the jars and filled each one with oil.

'Give me another jar,' she said to her son.

'There are none left,' he told her. Then the oil stopped flowing. She had many jars full of oil.

The woman returned to Elisha and told him what had happened.

'Now go and sell the oil. You will be able to pay your debt and you and your sons can stay together.'

176 THE GIFT OF A CHILD

Whenever Elisha passed through Shunem, a rich woman there offered him a meal and somewhere to stay. She and her husband had prepared a room for him on their roof. The room had a bed, a table, a chair and a lamp.

One day, when Elisha was staying at their house, he told his servant, Gehazi, to ask the woman to come to see him.

'You have been very kind to me,' Elisha said. 'Is there anything I can do to show my thanks?'

The woman shook her head. She felt she had all she needed. Elisha's servant saw that the woman's husband was old, and she had no child to look after her. He told Elisha that she might want a son.

'This time next year you will hold your baby son in your arms,' Elisha told her.

The woman was anxious; she did not want her hopes raised. Everything happened just as Elisha had said. A year later the woman gave birth to a baby boy.

177 THE MIRACLE OF THE SHUNAMMITE'S SON

The rich woman from Shunem loved her son dearly. Her life was completely different now God had blessed her.

One day the boy was out with his father at harvest time when suddenly he complained of pains in his head. His father sent him home in the arms of a servant. His mother took the boy on her lap and nursed him, but at midday, her son died.

The woman carried him up to Elisha's room and laid him on the bed. Then she asked her husband for a donkey and one of the servants so she could visit Elisha at Mount Carmel.

When Elisha saw her coming, he was worried. He asked Gehazi to go to meet her and ask what was wrong.

She would not tell him, but when she reached Elisha, she threw herself at his feet and took hold of him.

'Why did you give me a son just to take him away? I could live with the pain of having no child, but I cannot live with the agony of loving him and having him die!'

Elisha was very concerned. He went back with the woman and prayed to God to restore the boy. Then he breathed into his mouth and warmed him with his own body. He went out of the room, returned and did the same thing again.

Then the boy sneezed seven times. He opened his eyes. Elisha called the woman into the room.

'Here is your son,' said Elisha to the woman.

178 THE CAPTIVE SERVANT GIRL

In the land of Aram, an Israelite girl had been taken captive in one of the raids on nearby villages.

She worked as a servant in the home of an army commander called Naaman.

Naaman was a brave soldier and highly thought of. His skin was covered in the deadly white patches of leprosy.

'I wish my master could see the prophet in Samaria!' the Israelite girl told her mistress. 'I am sure he would cure his leprosy.'

Naaman went to the king of Aram and told him what the girl had said. The king then wrote a letter to King Joram of Israel and sent Naaman with silver, gold and other gifts.

'I am sending Naaman to you with this letter so that you can cure him of his leprosy,' the letter said.

King Joram was upset at the letter. He thought it was a trick so that the king of Aram could wage war on him. He didn't think of Elisha; he didn't consider that God could help him.

Elisha heard of King Joram's distress.

'Send him to me,' Elisha said. 'Then he will know that there is a prophet who serves God in Israel.'

179 NAAMAN IS CURED

Naaman went with his servants, his horses and his chariots, and stopped outside the place where Elisha lived. A servant came out from Elisha's house with a message from the prophet.

'Go to the River Jordan and wash there seven times.'

Naaman was angry. Elisha had not even come out to greet him.

'Surely there are better rivers in Damascus where I could wash!' he said. 'I thought he would come and wave his hand over my skin and pray to his God.'

One of his servants reasoned with Naaman.

'Sir,' he said, 'if the prophet had asked you to do something difficult, you would have done it. Don't be too proud to do this simple thing.'

Naaman listened and decided to go down to the River Jordan and wash. When he came out of the river the seventh time, his skin was clean and new and unmarked, like that of a child. He was cured.

'Now I know there is no God in all the world, except in Israel,' he said.

180 JEHU IS ANOINTED KING

The time had come for King Ahab's family to die, just as Elijah had prophesied. No one in Ahab's family remembered or obeyed God.

Elisha sent one of the young prophets on a mission.

'Take this bottle of oil, and find Jehu, the son of Jehoshaphat,' he said. 'Ask to speak to him secretly, and then anoint him king of Israel. Don't wait to explain further. Come back as fast as you can.'

The prophet found Jehu and drew him away from his companions. Once they were on their own, the prophet poured the oil on Jehu's head.

'God has chosen you to be the king of Israel. You must kill all who remain in Ahab's family, as punishment for their disobedience.' Then the prophet fled.

'What did he want?' asked one of the soldiers when Jehu returned.

'Nothing that makes much sense,' he replied. When his friends pressed him further, he told them. 'God has anointed me king.'

The men took off their cloaks and spread them on the steps under Jehu's feet. They blew on the trumpet and shouted:

'Jehu is king!'

181 THE DREADFUL END OF QUEEN JEZEBEL

The kings of Israel and Judah, Joram and Ahaziah, were both in Jezreel. Jehu gathered his troops and set out to find them.

The lookout on the watchtower saw his chariot approaching.

King Joram sent a soldier out on horseback to meet him and find out what he wanted. When the man caught up with him, Jehu told him to follow behind him. A second soldier was sent out, but Jehu made him follow behind as well.

'The man leading the troops is driving his chariot like a lunatic!' the lookout reported. 'Only Jehu drives like that!'

So King Joram of Israel and King Ahaziah of Judah went out to meet Jehu, each in their own chariot at the place that used to be Naboth's field.

'Have you come in peace?' asked King Joram.

'How can there be peace while your mother, Queen Jezebel, rules us with witchcraft and idol worship?' demanded Jehu.

'Treason!' King Joram shouted.

Jehu aimed his arrow and killed Joram with a single shot while Jehu's men pursued and wounded Ahaziah so that he died later.

Queen Jezebel was still in Jezreel. She painted her eyes and watched for Jehu from a window in the palace.

'What are you doing here, you murderer?' she demanded.

Jehu looked around to see who was on his side. He appealed to some palace officials.

'Throw her down!' he called.

The men took hold of Jezebel and threw her out of the window so that she fell to her death.

Ahab's family were dead; their rule was ended. King Jehu was free to rule Israel as God intended.

182 JEHU'S TRICK

King Jehu knew that there were still many worshippers of Baal in the land. He went to Samaria and called them all together for a feast.

'You know how well King Ahab served the god Baal,' he told the people. 'Well, now you will see how well I can serve him. Let all Baal's priests and all those who worship him come together here for a celebration. Anyone who does not come will be found and put to death!'

All the Baal worshippers came to the temple so that it was filled from end to end. Jehu made sure that no one who worshipped the one true God was there.

Then Jehu ordered his soldiers to put to death all those who were inside. He destroyed the sacred pillar inside the temple and then the temple itself. In this way he made sure that the evil of Ahab's family was wiped out from the land of Israel for ever.

183 A WICKED GRANDMOTHER

In Judah, Athaliah, the queen mother, ruled for six years. She had systematically killed the entire royal family after her son's death, so that no one could take power from her or challenge her right to rule.

Her baby grandson, Joash, had escaped. He was taken to the temple where Athaliah would never find him. A priest called Jehoiada looked after him there and as Joash grew up, he taught him all about God.

In the seventh year, Jehoiada secretly sent for the palace and temple guard and asked for their support. Then he put the crown on Joash's head and a copy of God's law in his hands. He made sure the guards surrounded him with their swords drawn.

'Stay close to your king,' he ordered the guards, as they led Joash out to face the people. Then he proclaimed Joash king of Judah.

The crowd that had gathered cheered and shouted.

'Long live the king!'

Athaliah came to see what all the noise was about. When she saw that Joash was alive and had been made king, she was furious.

'Treason!' she cried.

The people had a new king. No one listened to her now.

Jehoiada made sure Athaliah was removed from the celebrations and then executed at the Horse Gate, out of the way of the crowds and of her grandson. Joash was seven years old when he became king.

184 JOASH REPAIRS THE TEMPLE

Jehoiada made sure the people knew that everything would now be different in Judah. The people came back to God and renewed their covenant with him so that they would once more be his people and he would be their God.

The altars and the idols of Baal were smashed. The temple of Baal was destroyed as it had been in Israel.

Joash had listened to everything Jehoiada had taught him about God. He told the priests to collect money from the people so that the temple could be repaired.

Jehoiada found a large chest. He made a hole in the top of it, and put it by the side of the altar for the people to put money in. Then when it was full, the silver would be melted down and weighed and used to pay the carpenters, masons and stone cutters. It would also buy the wood and stone needed to make the repairs.

So work began to repair the temple, and Joash tried to lead his people back towards God.

185 THE DEATH OF ELISHA

In Israel, Jehu's son, Jehoahaz, became king and after him, his son, Jehoash. During this time the prophet Elisha became very ill.

King Jehoash went to Elisha and wept. He knew that Elisha had served God faithfully but also that he and his people had failed to do so.

Elisha spoke to the king from his bed.

'Take some arrows and shoot out of the window towards Syria,' he said. The king did so.

'You are the Lord's arrow,' Elisha told him. 'You will fight and defeat the Syrians.'

Then Elisha told the king to strike the ground with the other arrows. The king did so three times.

'If only you had struck the ground five or six times!' said Elisha. 'You will defeat the Syrians, but only three times, not completely.'

Elisha died and was buried.

Time passed, and king after king in Israel turned from God and failed to obey him. Evil men had power, and the people worshipped the gods of the nations around them again.

186 JONAH RUNS AWAY

The Assyrians were a growing threat to God's people. Their country bordered the lands of Israel to the north, and they were greedy to take more land for themselves and become even more powerful.

So when God called on Jonah, one of his prophets, to go to Nineveh and warn them to repent of their wickedness, he was not happy. What had Israel's God to do with the Assyrians?

Jonah was so unhappy that he went to the port of Joppa to look for a ship going to Tarshish, about as far in the opposite direction as he could go…

Jonah paid his fare, boarded the ship and then went below deck where he fell into a deep sleep.

187 THE RAGING STORM

The ship had not long been out to sea when the wind grew stronger and a violent storm arose. Waves battered the sides of the ship and it lurched so dangerously that the sailors on board were sure they would drown.

The men prayed to their gods and threw their cargo over the side to lighten the ship. They clung to one another in fear.

Then the captain noticed that Jonah was missing. He went below deck to find him.

'Wake up!' he cried, shaking Jonah. 'How can you sleep through this storm? Get up and pray! Perhaps your God can save us.'

By this time the sailors were sure that the storm was someone's fault. They drew lots to see who was responsible. Then they stood back and stared at Jonah. It was clear that he was the guilty one.

'What terrible thing have you done that your God is punishing us?' they asked Jonah. 'Who are you?'

'I worship the God who made the land and the sea,' Jonah replied. 'I have run away from him. This is all my fault. There is only one thing you can do: you must throw me overboard.'

188 MAN OVERBOARD!

The sailors listened in horror. They did not want to kill Jonah, but they did not want to die either.

At first they tried to row back to shore, but the sea was too strong for them.

'Do not blame us for taking this man's life!' the sailors prayed.

They picked up Jonah and threw him over the side.

The wind dropped straight away; the waves grew calm. The sailors were amazed and fell to their knees. They had seen the power of the living God.

Jonah, meanwhile, had sunk beneath the waves and felt himself falling down, down, down and strangled by seaweed. Then, as he felt his life draining away from him, he called to God for help, and God answered.

God sent a huge fish to swallow him whole, and saved him.

Jonah stayed inside the body of the fish for three days and three nights. He thought about what had happened and how he had tried to run away from God. He remembered that he had once promised to serve God and do whatever he asked, and he praised God and promised to serve him again because only God had the power to save.

Then God spoke to the huge fish and commanded it to spit Jonah out on to dry land.

189 THE GOD WHO FORGIVES

God had given Jonah a second chance. This time when God said, 'Go to Nineveh,' Jonah went.

Jonah went through the streets of the great city and he preached the message that God had given him. He warned the people that they must ask for God's forgiveness and change their ways, or their land would be destroyed in 40 days.

The people did not need to be told more than once. They heard what Jonah said and they believed his message. Even the king listened and acted.

'No one is to eat or drink. Everyone must wear sackcloth and ask God to forgive them. Everyone must stop doing evil and violent things. Perhaps even now it is possible that God may change his mind and forgive us.'

God watched the people of Nineveh and he heard their prayers. Because God was compassionate, he forgave them. He did not destroy the people of Assyria.

190 JONAH'S ANGER

Jonah was furious that God had listened to the prayers of the Assyrians.

'I knew this would happen,' he said angrily. 'I knew you were kind and forgiving and that you would love these people if they changed their ways. That's why I ran away! They are evil people and they deserve to die. Now I might as well be dead!'

Jonah went outside the city and sulked. God let a vine grow over his head to give him shade from the hot sun. The next day, a worm ate the vine so that it died and Jonah grew weak from the heat.

'Let me die!' he cried to God.

Then God spoke to Jonah.

'Why are you so angry? I let the vine grow, and I let the vine die. You are unhappy about the death of the vine even though you did nothing to help it grow and did not look after it. It is only a vine, but still you are angry. Now try to understand how I feel about the thousands of people who live in the city of Nineveh. They hardly know right from wrong. I made these people. I know them and care about them. I do not want them to die, Jonah. You mustn't be angry because I choose to save them.'

191 THE GOD OF THE POOR

During the time when Uzziah was king of Judah, there lived a shepherd called Amos who also looked after the fig trees.

'Amos,' God said, 'I want you to give my people a message. Go to them and speak for me.'

'Be warned!' Amos said to his own people in Judah. 'God has seen what you do. You are no different from other nations. Although you know God's laws, you don't keep them. You have sinned again and again. For this you will be punished and Jerusalem will be burned to the ground.'

Then Amos spoke to the people of Israel.

'Be warned! You are God's people and he cares for you. Yet you ignore God's laws and you worship idols. You have plenty of money and enjoy many possessions but you have become rich by oppressing and cheating the poor people around you. Change your ways! Put what you believe into practice. Learn to love what is good and hate what is evil.

'This is what God says: "You offer me gifts when you come to worship me; you sing noisy songs and play your harps. I will accept none of this. I would rather you lived your lives in the right way, being fair and kind to those around you. Let justice flow like a stream through a dry land and righteousness like a river that never runs dry."'

Then God gave Amos a vision of a wall beside a plumb line.

'I will put a plumb line in the middle of my people. I will judge them and see that they are not like a wall that is built straight and true but instead they are crooked and out of line. The time is coming soon when they will lose what they have and be taken from their homes into exile in a foreign land.'

192 THE LOVING HUSBAND

Then God chose another man, Hosea, to be his messenger.

'Your whole life will be a picture for my people in Israel,' said God. 'I want you to marry a woman who will make you sad. She will leave you and love other men. She won't care how much you love her and she will forget all about you whatever you do for her, but you will not leave her. You will keep on loving her.'

So Hosea married Gomer, and they had children. Gomer left him for another man and eventually she became a slave.

'Now go and get your wife back,' said God. 'Buy her out of slavery. Live with her and keep on loving her.'

Hosea paid the price to get his wife back, and he loved her.

'I love the people of Israel just as much as you love Gomer,' explained God. 'My people have hurt me and made me sad. They have ignored me and left me for other things. I have not left them. They will be punished, but I will keep on loving them.'

193 THE PROMISE OF PEACE

It was about this time that the prophet Micah brought God's message to the people of Israel, warning them of the coming invasion of the Assyrians.

'You have rebelled against God!' said Micah. 'You are supposed to be concerned about justice, yet you hate what is good and go about doing evil. Soon you will call out to God for help, but it will be too late! All your idols will be destroyed; everything will be smashed to pieces. Your enemies will defeat you and you will be taken away from your home to be exiles in a foreign land.'

Micah also promised that there would be a time after God's punishment when he would bring someone to save them.

'God says to Bethlehem: "You are one of the smallest towns in Judah, but I will bring from your people a ruler for Israel. You will be defeated by your enemies until a woman gives birth to her son. Then those who have remained faithful will come together. God will stand among his people. He will lead them and care for them as a shepherd cares for his sheep, and there will be peace.

'Do you know what God wants of you? Do you know how to live so you can please him? You must act with justice, you must always be kind and you must be humble before God, your maker.'

194 ISAIAH'S VISION

At the end of the reign of King Uzziah, God also spoke to the people through the prophet Isaiah.

Isaiah was in the temple when he had a vision of God and knew that God was calling him to serve him. Isaiah wrote down what he saw.

'God sat upon his throne, high and exalted, and the folds of his robe filled the temple. Round him were heavenly creatures, each of which had six wings. With two wings they covered their faces; with two wings they covered their feet; and with two wings they flew.

'They called out to each other, saying, "Holy, holy, holy! The Lord God almighty is holy!"

'The foundations of the temple shook at the sound of their voices and the temple filled with smoke.

'I felt so sinful, so unworthy, to be in God's holy presence and to know that I and all my people were so far from the holiness of the God whom we claimed to know and worship.

'Then one of the heavenly creatures flew down to me carrying a burning coal from the altar. He touched my lips with it and said, "Your guilt is gone; your sin is forgiven."

'Then I heard the voice of God: "Whom shall I send?" he asked. "Who will take my words to the people?"

'I answered: "I will go! Send me!"'

195 THE FUTURE KING

God sent Isaiah to his people with a message.

'God has seen all the terrible things you have done and no one will escape God's punishment. Time is running out. Turn away from your wrongdoing now,' Isaiah told the people of Judah. 'Tell God how sorry you are before it is too late.'

No one wanted to hear bad news. Isaiah also had good news. He told them about a time in the future when God would do something very wonderful.

'God will punish his people because they will not listen to him, but he will not be angry for ever. God will remember his people.

'God will give to his people his son. A child will be born who will rule over all people with justice and righteousness. He will bring light into dark places. He will bring peace that lasts for ever.

'He will be called "Wonderful Counsellor", "Mighty God", "Eternal Father" and "Prince of Peace". He will be born into the family of King David, and God's own Spirit will be with him.'

196 ISRAEL FALLS TO THE ASSYRIANS

When Hoshea became king of Israel, King Shalmaneser of Assyria attacked Israel and defeated Hoshea's army. Hoshea was allowed to remain king as long as Israel paid heavy taxes to Assyria.

Hoshea tried to plot against Shalmaneser with the help of the king of Egypt. He asked him to be his ally, so that together they could overthrow the Assyrians. The plot was discovered, and the Assyrian army poured into Israel. Shalmaneser arrested King Hoshea and had him put in prison. Then he marched on towards Samaria where the people defended themselves for three years under siege before they were defeated.

King Shalmaneser captured the people of Israel, and had them taken away to Assyria. Then he filled the land that God had given to the Israelites with people from other tribes, who bowed down to gods of wood and stone.

The warnings given by the prophets had begun to come true. God's people were being punished for rebelling against God and not following his ways.

197 HEZEKIAH TRUSTS GOD

In Judah, there was a king at last who loved God. Hezekiah destroyed all the idols and places of pagan worship in the land and trusted God to help him and his people.

Hezekiah defeated the Philistines, and unlike the people of Israel, he refused to pay the Assyrians the taxes they demanded. The Assyrian army swept through Israel, conquering some of Judah's major towns.

'Surrender to Assyria!' shouted Sennacherib's official. 'Don't listen to King Hezekiah! Your God is no different from the gods of all the nations around you. He has no power. He cannot save you.'

Hezekiah put on sackcloth and prayed. He asked the prophet Isaiah for advice.

'God says you must trust him. He will cause the commander to hear a rumour that will make him return to his own country, and there he will be killed.'

It happened just as God had told Isaiah. Then Hezekiah prayed.

'Almighty Lord, you alone are God. You created the earth and the sky. Now, Lord, rescue us from the Assyrians, so that all the nations of the world will know that you alone are God.'

'God has answered your prayer,' said Isaiah. 'The Assyrians will not enter the city, nor even shoot an arrow. God will defend us.'

An angel went to the Assyrian camp and that night, 185,000 soldiers died. Sennacherib returned home to Nineveh where he was killed by two of his sons.

198 THE SHADOW OF THE SUNDIAL

Some time later, King Hezekiah became very ill.

'It is time for you to die,' the prophet Isaiah told him. 'Make sure you have put everything in order.'

King Hezekiah turned to face the wall, weeping.

'Lord God, please remember me. Know that I have tried to serve you as best as I could.'

As Isaiah left the palace, he heard God speaking to him again.

'Give Hezekiah this message. I have seen his tears and heard his prayer. I will let him live for another 15 years.'

Isaiah rushed back to tell the king and told his attendants to put a paste made out of figs on the inflammation on his body.

'How can I be sure?' Hezekiah asked Isaiah. 'Will God give me a sign?'

'Do you want the shadow of the sundial to move ten steps backwards or forwards?' asked Isaiah.

'Backwards!' exclaimed Hezekiah. 'It always moves forwards.'

So Isaiah prayed. The shadow of the sundial moved backwards. Hezekiah went to the temple to praise and worship God.

Hezekiah built more cities and channelled the water from the Spring of Gihon so that it flowed through a tunnel into Jerusalem to provide fresh water. When he died, Hezekiah was buried in the tomb of the kings.

199 WORDS OF HOPE

God gave messages of hope and comfort to Isaiah to pass on to his people.

'"Comfort my people," says our God. "Tell them that they have suffered long enough and now I will forgive them."

'God himself is coming to rule his people. He will take care of them as a shepherd takes care of his sheep. He will gather the lambs together and carry them gently in his arms.

'How can we describe our God? Can we take the ocean and measure it in our hands? Can we take all the soil from the earth and put it in a cup? Can we pick up a mountain and weigh it in the scales?

'At the beginning of time, God stretched out the sky like a curtain; he led out the stars like an army and counted them.

'Do you think God doesn't know about your troubles? Do you believe he doesn't care if you suffer? Haven't you heard about him? The Lord is the eternal God: he created the whole world. He doesn't grow tired or weary. Instead he helps and supports all those who are weak. Anyone who puts their trust in God will find new strength. They will rise on wings like eagles; they will run and not get tired; they will walk and not grow weak.'

200 GOD'S LOVE FOR HIS PEOPLE

Another time Isaiah spoke to the people about God's love for them.

'Listen, people of Israel, to what the God who created you says: "Do not be afraid because I will save you. I have called you by your name; you belong to me.

'"When you pass through deep waters, I will be with you. I will not let the flood waters overwhelm you. When you walk through fire, I will not let you be burned. The flames will not destroy you.

'"I am the Lord your God, the holy one of Israel, who will save you. You are precious to me and I love you.

'"Come to me, everyone who is thirsty. I have cool water for you. Come to me, everyone who has no money. I have a feast to share with you. Why do you want to spend your money on things that cannot satisfy you? Why buy things that leave you hungry again tomorrow? Come to me and listen. Come to me and I will give you life!"'

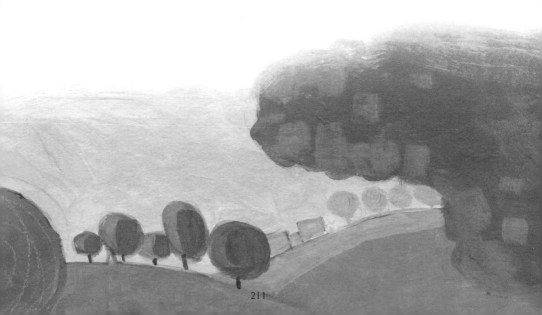

201 GOD'S PLAN TO SAVE HIS PEOPLE

Isaiah also told the people about the child God had promised to send.

'This child will be rejected by his people. He will suffer and know pain. His pain will be our pain; he will suffer in our place. He will die because we have sinned, not for any sin of his own. He will take the punishment that we deserved for our sins, so that we can be forgiven.

'We are all like sheep that are lost, each wandering away from the right path and going our own way. He will be like a lamb that goes to be slaughtered; like a sheep waiting to be sheared. He will be arrested and sentenced to death; he will be led away to die though he is innocent of any crime.

'It is God's will that he should suffer for us; he will go to his death willingly in our place. After all he suffers, he will again have joy. He will know that his death has achieved something good. His one death will save many.'

202 KING MANASSEH'S PUNISHMENT

Hezekiah's son, Manasseh, became king after his father's death. Instead of worshipping God, he started to worship the sun, the moon and the stars. He sacrificed his own son to foreign gods and practised witchcraft. He brought idols into God's temple and slaughtered many innocent people.

Manasseh would not listen to the warnings of the prophets God sent to him. So when the Assyrians attacked Judah, they took Manasseh prisoner. They humiliated him and put a hook in his nose; they bound him in bronze chains, and took him to Babylon.

Only after all his suffering did Manasseh remember God and how he had disobeyed him.

'I have been wicked! I am so sorry for all the things I have done,' he cried. Then he asked God to forgive him.

God heard Manasseh's prayer. God let him return to Jerusalem where he destroyed the altars and the idols he had made. Then Manasseh told the people that they must follow God's ways.

Some of the people listened, but others, including his own son, Amon, who became king after him, continued to sin. They rejected God and disobeyed his commandments.

203 KING JOSIAH'S SORROW

After a plot against him, Amon was assassinated. His son, Josiah, was only eight when he was made king of Judah.

Josiah wanted to serve God as King David had done. He repaired the temple so that the people could worship God again.

When the work was under way, the high priest, Hilkiah, discovered an old scroll which contained the covenant God had made with his people and the prophecy of the destruction of Jerusalem because of the people's disobedience. When Josiah heard the laws written on the scroll, he wept and tore his clothes.

'Pray to God. Find out what God wants us to do. We have broken all of his laws. He must be so angry with us.'

Hilkiah hurried to find the prophetess, Huldah.

'God says that he will destroy Jerusalem,' she said. 'But God has also seen the king's sorrow. It won't happen in Josiah's lifetime.'

Josiah summoned the people to the temple.

'I promise to serve God with all my heart,' declared Josiah. 'We promise too,' declared the people.

Josiah destroyed all the idols and altars to foreign gods. Then he led the people in celebrating the Passover. Josiah served God with all his heart, all his mind and all his strength, and he obeyed God's commandments.

204 GOD'S CHOSEN MESSENGER

The evil of King Manasseh could not easily be forgotten. There would be peace in Josiah's time, but not for those who came after him. When Josiah had been king for twelve years, God spoke to a priest's teenage son, Jeremiah.

'Before you were conceived in your mother's womb, I knew you, Jeremiah. Before you were born, I chose you and set you apart to be my messenger.'

Jeremiah could hardly believe God's words.

'I'm only a child,' he answered. 'I don't know how to serve you and be your prophet!'

'I will tell you what you must say,' said God. 'You must not be afraid. I will be with you and I will keep you safe.'

Then Jeremiah felt a hand touch his lips.

'I have put my words in your mouth,' said God. 'Speak for me.'

A picture started to form before Jeremiah's eyes and in his vision he saw a pot, full of a scalding, boiling liquid. It was tilting towards the south and the burning liquid was ready to gush out.

'The people of Judah have been disobedient. They have worshipped idols; they have not obeyed my laws. Soon they will be destroyed by an enemy from the north,' said God.

'Now Jeremiah, go and tell them what you have seen. They will be angry; they will not want to hear it, but remember that I am with you.'

205 A REBELLIOUS PEOPLE

Jeremiah went to the people of Jerusalem with God's words.

'I remember when I first brought you out of Egypt,' said God. 'You were my people and I was your God. You loved and trusted me and I protected you from your enemies.

'What went wrong? What made your ancestors turn from me to worthless idols? When they were in trouble, I was there to help them. They needed only to ask and I would rescue them. Instead, they chose gods made out of wood and stone rather than the God who made them and the world they live in. Now you are in real trouble. Where are your gods now? Let them save you if they can!

'It's not too late to be sorry and keep the covenant we had. Act now! Turn from your wicked ways and love me again. Soon it will be too late. Your enemy in the north is preparing for battle. His war chariots are coming like a whirlwind; his horses are faster than eagles and will swoop down and devour you. They have taken up their bows and swords; they are cruel and without mercy. Change your ways now. You have brought the disaster upon yourselves, but it is not too late to turn back to me.'

Jeremiah wept for the people. He went to them time and time again and warned them of the punishment that was awaiting them. He told them that God would listen if they came back and said sorry. The people laughed at Jeremiah. They would not believe what he said.

206 THE POTTER'S CLAY

One day, God told Jeremiah to go to watch the potter at his wheel. He moulded a lump of clay, cupping his wet hands around it, pulling the clay into the shape of a pot. Suddenly the wheel stopped spinning. The potter was unhappy with the shape of the pot. He picked up the clay, threw it back on the wheel and began to reshape it into something better.

'I am like that potter,' said God. 'My people are like the clay. If they are rebellious and disobedient, then I will start again. I will reshape them into something useful and perfect. The people of Judah will suffer, and the suffering will shape them into the people I want them to be.'

Then God told Jeremiah to buy a clay pot and go out to the Valley of Hinnom with some of the elders and priests. There he was to warn them about the terrible things that were to happen.

'God's people have filled this place with the blood of innocent people,' Jeremiah told them. 'Now God will punish them. Soon this will be called the Valley of Slaughter. The enemy will come and besiege the city and the suffering will be so terrible that the people will eat one another.'

Then Jeremiah smashed the clay pot in front of the men.

'This is what God says he will do to this rebellious people,' he said. 'They will be broken in so many pieces that they cannot be put back together.'

Still the people did not believe Jeremiah. Pashhur the priest had him beaten and chained up by one of the gates in the temple.

207 JEREMIAH BUYS A FIELD

The Babylonians were making attacks on Jerusalem when God told Jeremiah to buy a field from his cousin, Hanamel.

So when Jeremiah received a visit from his cousin, he bought the field and had the papers signed, sealed and witnessed. Jeremiah did not understand. Why buy land when God had said that everything would be destroyed?

'Lord God,' said Jeremiah. 'I know that nothing is impossible for you, but why did you want me to buy that field?'

'It is a sign of what will happen,' said God. 'Jerusalem will be destroyed, because my people have refused to listen to me. One day, some of them will return. They will come back to live here, and fields will once more be bought and sold. This is my promise for the future. I will look after my people. I will give them good things, and I will be their God.'

208 THE WORDS IN THE FIRE

When Jehoiakim was king of Judah, the prophecies about the destruction of Jerusalem began to come true. The attacks made on Judah by King Nebuchadnezzar of Babylon became more fierce. Still no one took Jeremiah seriously.

'Buy a scroll,' said God to Jeremiah, 'and write down everything I have ever told you.'

Jeremiah dictated everything to Baruch, who wrote Jeremiah's words down on the scroll.

'Take this scroll to the temple,' said Jeremiah. 'I have been banned from going there. Read this out to the people.'

Baruch went and read from the scroll. When Jehudi heard about it, he told Baruch to come and read it to him and the other court officials. Then they were terrified. They realised the warning must be taken seriously.

'We must tell the king,' they said. 'You and Jeremiah must hide.'

It was winter, and King Jehoiakim was sitting by an open fire as Jehudi unrolled the scroll and read to him. He had read only a few columns before Jehoiakim told him to stop. The king took a knife, cut the words from the scroll and threw them carelessly into the fire. The more Jehudi read, the more Jehoiakim cut and threw into the flames, until the whole scroll was burned.

'Start again,' said God to Jeremiah. 'Write on another scroll. I will punish Jehoiakim because he has refused to listen to me.'

209 THE BABYLONIANS TAKE CAPTIVES

Nothing could stop the Babylonians from attacking Judah. They captured officials, builders and craftsmen. They captured King Jehoiakim and took him away to Babylon in chains. King Nebuchadnezzar stripped the palace and took away many of the beautiful treasures from the temple.

Then, in the spring, the Babylonians returned. All the remaining treasures were taken from the temple. Jehoiachin, who was now king, was captured and taken to Babylon, along with 10,000 others. Among these was a man called Ezekiel.

Once they were captives in a foreign land, the people remembered the words of warning the prophets had given them. They wished they had listened. They began to be sorry that they had disobeyed God. The people who were left unharmed in Jerusalem thought they had escaped God's punishment. Despite what had happened, they were pleased with themselves.

Nebuchadnezzar made Zedekiah king of Judah.

Jeremiah was one of those left behind in Jerusalem. One day he was near the temple.

'Look at those two baskets of figs,' said God. 'What can you see?'

'One basket is full of good, ripe figs,' replied Jeremiah. 'The other figs are rotten. They are fit for nothing.'

'Think about those figs,' said God. 'The people who are in captivity in Babylon are like the good figs. I will look after them. The rotten figs are like King Zedekiah and all those who are left behind in Jerusalem. They are so bad that they are not fit to be saved.'

210 JEREMIAH IN PRISON

Day after day, the soldiers camped outside Jerusalem while inside, food became scarce. Zedekiah asked Jeremiah to pray for help.

'The Babylonians will retreat when they see that the Egyptians are coming to help you,' said God. 'But they will return and burn down the city. Only those who surrender will be safe.'

Knowing that the enemy had retreated for a while, Jeremiah went to look at the field that God had told him to buy.

'Why are you leaving?' demanded one of the soldiers. 'You traitor! You are going to join the Babylonians!'

He had Jeremiah beaten and imprisoned. He was still in prison when King Zedekiah asked if there were any messages from God.

'God has said that you will be handed over to the Babylonians,' Jeremiah told him. 'Please don't send me back to prison!'

Zedekiah had Jeremiah locked up in the palace courtyard instead, and Jeremiah continued to warn the people.

'Surrender and escape with your life! Stay and you will die of starvation or disease! God is punishing his people because they have turned from him to foreign idols.'

'Stop that man!' the officials told the king. 'He is spreading fear among the soldiers. How can they put up a fight when he tells them there is no hope left?'

King Zedekiah waved them away.

'Do what you like with him!' he said.

211 AT THE BOTTOM OF THE WELL

Jeremiah was thrown into the well. There was no water there, and he sank down into the mud. As he sat in the darkness, he thought he was going to die.

Ebed-Melech, one of the king's officials, heard what had happened.

'Your majesty,' he said. 'Jeremiah will die if he is left in the well.'

King Zedekiah was weary.

'Bring him out before he dies,' he said.

So Ebed-Melech found some rope and some worn-out clothing and some men to help him. He made sure Jeremiah put the clothing under his arms so the rope would not hurt him, and gently hauled Jeremiah up out of the well and into the light.

212 THE FALL OF JERUSALEM

'Tell me what you know!' said King Zedekiah. 'What will happen to me?'

'I have told you many times,' said Jeremiah, 'but you do not listen. Surrender or you and your family will die.'

'I'm afraid!' wailed Zedekiah. 'What will they do to me?'

'If you obey God, you will live,' Jeremiah reassured him.

Zedekiah did not listen. The Babylonians laid siege to Jerusalem once more. The people were starving. King Zedekiah tried to escape by leaving at night through the royal garden.

The Babylonians chased after the king and took him captive. They killed his sons in front of him, executed his officials and then blinded him. They bound him with chains and took him to Babylon, where he remained in prison until he died.

The Babylonians raided the temple of anything left that was valuable and could be carried away. They set fire to all the buildings and broke down the city walls. They put the people in chains and took them away to Babylon. Only a few poor people were left behind to work in the fields.

A captain in the Babylonian guard saw Jeremiah, who was in chains.

'All this happened just as you said it would, because your people ignored your God,' said the captain. 'I will let you go free. You can come with me to Babylon, or you can stay here if you prefer.'

Jeremiah knew that God had kept his promise and kept him safe. Jeremiah made his decision. He chose to stay with the people who were left in his homeland.

213 CAPTIVES IN BABYLON

The captives who had been taken to Babylon were not treated badly. King Nebuchadnezzar asked his chief officer to select some of the best young men to be educated and trained to work for him in the palace.

Among those chosen were four young men from the royal palace in Judah: Daniel, Hananiah, Mishael and Azariah. They were given new names, Belteshazzar, Shadrach, Meshach and Abednego, and given food and wine from the king's own table. They were to be trained for three years.

Daniel was unhappy. Although he was a captive in a strange land, he did not want to eat any of the foods which were forbidden by God. He asked the king's chief officer to give him only water to drink and vegetables to eat.

'The king himself has decided what you must eat to make you fit and healthy,' he answered. 'I will lose my life as well as my job if you fall ill!'

So Daniel spoke instead to the guard.

'We won't fall ill. Try it and see. Give us just water and vegetables. If we look weak after ten days, then we will eat whatever you give us.'

The guard agreed, and when, ten days later, Daniel and his friends looked healthier than the other young men, they were allowed to eat the food they had chosen. Then God blessed them and gave them special abilities, so that they were the best among the captives who had been chosen. God also gave to Daniel the ability to understand dreams and visions.

When the four young men had finished their training, they were presented to King Nebuchadnezzar. He was amazed at their wisdom and understanding.

214 NEBUCHADNEZZAR'S DREAM

King Nebuchadnezzar did not sleep well. His mind was troubled and he had strange dreams that worried him. He called his magicians and astrologers and told them the problem.

'Tell me what I dreamed and what it means, so that I will once more be able to sleep!' said the king.

'Tell us your dream and we will explain it to you,' his wise men replied.

The king became angry. 'No! I will reward the man who tells me what I dreamed and its meaning. If you cannot, then you will all be killed!'

'It's impossible!' they cried. 'There is no man on earth who can do what you ask.'

So Nebuchadnezzar sent them away and ordered the execution of all the wise men in his service.

When the king's official came to find Daniel and his friends to carry out the execution, Daniel asked what had happened to make the king issue such an order. Then he went to King Nebuchadnezzar and asked for more time to interpret the dream.

'Pray!' Daniel urged his friends. 'We must ask God to reveal the king's dream to us, or we must die with all the wise men in Babylon.'

The four men prayed and asked God to help them, and during the night, God gave Daniel a vision so that the mystery was clear to him.

'We praise you, Lord God!' Daniel prayed. 'You are wise and powerful. You reveal things hidden in darkness, mysteries that no one can understand. You have answered my prayer and given me wisdom; you have made known to me the king's dream.'

215 THE MYSTERY REVEALED

The next day, Daniel went to the king.

'Can you tell me what I dreamed?' asked Nebuchadnezzar.

'Your majesty,' said Daniel, 'there is no wise man alive who can tell you what you dreamed, but there is a God in heaven who can reveal mysteries, and he has shown you what the future holds.

'You dreamed of a huge statue. Its head was made of gold, its chest and arms were made of silver, its belly and thighs were made of bronze, its legs were made of iron and its feet of iron and clay.

'Then out of a mountain, a rock was cut. It fell down and shattered the statue so that the gold and silver, the bronze, iron and clay, all lay in pieces. Then a wind came and blew it all away, while the rock became a mountain as big as the earth.

'This is what it means,' continued Daniel. 'God has given you everything you have and power over all you see around you. You are the golden head of the statue. After you will come other powerful kingdoms, but in time they will all fall away.

'The rock that became a mountain is the kingdom that God will make, greater than any of them; it will never end.'

King Nebuchadnezzar fell at Daniel's feet.

'Your God is the true God!' he cried. 'He is the king of all kings!'

Then King Nebuchadnezzar gave Daniel gifts and made him ruler over the province of Babylon and all the wise men in the kingdom. Daniel gave Shadrach, Meshach and Abednego important jobs in the province, while he continued to stay in the palace.

216 THE GOLDEN STATUE

King Nebuchadnezzar made a huge statue of gold. It was placed on an open plain in Babylon and was so tall and wide that it could be seen for miles around.

Nebuchadnezzar called everyone of any importance in the provinces to stand before the statue.

A herald stood up and made an announcement.

'The king has commanded all of you, whatever language you speak, to bow down and worship the golden statue that King Nebuchadnezzar has made. As soon as you hear the sound of music, you must bow down and worship. Anyone who fails to do this will be thrown into a blazing furnace of fire!'

The music sounded. Everyone fell down to worship the statue as they had been commanded; everyone except Shadrach, Meshach and Abednego.

217 THE BLAZING FURNACE

Some of the king's astrologers were troublemakers.

'Your majesty,' they said to the king, 'you have commanded that everyone worship the golden statue that stands on the plain. There are men to whom you have given power who do not obey you or worship your gods. Three Jews, Shadrach, Meshach and Abednego, refuse to bow down and worship the statue.'

The king sent for the three men who were Daniel's friends.

'You refuse to obey me,' the king said. 'I will give you one more chance. Worship the statue, or be thrown into the blazing furnace of fire. Then no god will be able to save you!'

'O king,' the friends replied, 'you are great, but our God is greater still. If you throw us into the fire, our God is able to save us. Yet whether he rescues us or not, we will worship only him.'

In a rage, the king ordered the three men be tied up and thrown into the fire while he watched.

'Were not three men tied up and thrown into the fire? Yet I can see four men walking around in freedom! Get them out!'

The three men stepped out of the fire, completely unharmed. Their clothing was not scorched; they did not even smell of smoke.

'Praise the living God!' exclaimed Nebuchadnezzar. 'He sent an angel to rescue you because you were prepared to die for him.'

Then Nebuchadnezzar issued another decree.

'No one must say anything against the God of Shadrach, Meshach and Abednego. For he alone has the power to save.'

218 THE MADNESS OF THE KING

King Nebuchadnezzar dreamed again and called all his advisers to help him. As before, none could help him except Daniel.

'I dreamed that I was looking at a tree that grew so tall that it touched the sky. It could be seen from all the ends of the earth. Its leaves were beautiful and it produced enough fruit for everyone to eat. It was so strong that all the creatures on earth sheltered under it, and all the birds lived in its branches.

'While I watched, an angel came from heaven, who called for the tree to be chopped down, its branches to be cut off, its leaves to be stripped and its fruit to be scattered. The animals fled from under it and the birds flew away. Its stump was bound with chains and it was drenched with dew.'

Daniel understood the meaning of the dream all too well, but he was afraid to tell the king.

'The dream is a nightmare, O King!' said Daniel. 'I wish it applied to someone other than you. You are that tree that has grown as tall as the sky so that all the nations around know how great and powerful you are.

'God has seen all this but now wants you to know that you are nothing compared to him. He wants you to change and do what is right. He wants you to be kind to those you have oppressed. Unless you do this, your mind will be destroyed, and you will live among the animals and eat grass like the cattle.'

It all happened as Daniel told the king. Nebuchadnezzar endured a time of madness. At the end of it, he realised that God was indeed the God of all the earth. He praised God and understood that he loved kindness and justice and hated oppression and cruelty.

219 THE WRITING ON THE WALL

When King Nebuchadnezzar died, Daniel and his friends were forgotten. Years later King Belshazzar gave a magnificent feast.

All the great men in Babylon were invited, and Belshazzar ordered that the wine be served in the gold and silver goblets stolen from the temple in Jerusalem. The men sang praises to the gods of gold and silver, bronze, iron, wood and stone.

Suddenly the fingers of a human hand appeared and started moving against the wall. One by one people stopped eating and drinking. Then the king went white and collapsed on the floor.

The fingers wrote: 'MENE, MENE, TEKEL, PARSIN.'

'Find someone to tell me what this means!' said Belshazzar weakly. 'I will make him the third most powerful person in the land.'

No one could tell him the meaning of the writing on the wall.

Then the Queen Mother remembered Daniel and sent for him.

'God sent this hand to write on the wall because he has seen your wickedness,' said Daniel. 'He has weighed you on the scales and you have been judged unworthy. Your rule is at an end. Your kingdom will be taken by the Medes and the Persians.'

Belshazzar knew he had heard the truth, but it was too late. That night the Persian army attacked Babylon. Belshazzar was killed.

220 A PLOT AGAINST DANIEL

When Darius the Mede became ruler, he saw that Daniel was gifted and experienced and made him one of his top three administrators.

Daniel worked hard and Darius was so impressed with him that he wanted to put Daniel in charge of the whole kingdom. There were other officials who were jealous of Daniel. They wanted to remove him from office; they wanted to find something—anything—that would make him lose his job.

'It's useless!' they said to one another. 'The only way we will ever get rid of Daniel is if it has something to do with his God.'

They plotted and schemed and slowly an idea began to take shape. They went to see Darius.

'Your majesty, may you live for ever!' they said. 'We all think that you are such a great king that you should issue a decree. No one must pray to anyone but you for the next 30 days. If they do, they should be thrown into a den of lions!'

Darius was flattered. It was a good idea, he thought. He even put it in writing so that it became law—and the law of the Medes and Persians cannot be changed.

221 DANIEL AND THE LIONS

When Daniel heard about the decree, he went as usual to his upstairs room where the windows faced Jerusalem. He knelt and prayed three times a day to God, asking him for help. The men who had plotted knew their plan had worked.

'Your majesty,' they said, 'are we right in thinking that anyone who disobeys your decree will be thrown into a den of lions?'

'This decree cannot be altered,' the king nodded.

'Daniel ignores the decree. He does not pray to you. Instead he prays three times a day to his God.'

Darius was very sad. He realised that the men had set out to trap him, and now he was powerless to rescue Daniel. Darius had no choice. He ordered Daniel to be thrown into the lions' den.

'May your God save you,' he said to Daniel.

That night Darius could not sleep. As soon as it was morning, he returned to the lions' den.

'Daniel!' he cried. 'Has your God saved you from the lions?'

'Yes, your majesty!' shouted Daniel from the den. 'He sent an angel to close the mouths of the hungry lions. I am unharmed.'

'Release Daniel!' cried Darius. 'And punish those men who have tried to hurt him.'

Then Darius issued another decree.

'All the people in my kingdom must respect Daniel's God, for he is the living God who performs signs and wonders. He has the power to save, even from the mouths of lions!'

Daniel continued faithful to God for the rest of his life.

222 A VISION OF GOD

Ezekiel was a priest. When Nebuchadnezzar attacked Jerusalem, Ezekiel had been taken captive and had settled with many other Jewish exiles on the banks of the Kebar River in Babylon.

One day God spoke to Ezekiel in a vision. Ezekiel saw a storm cloud moving towards him, with lightning flashing around it in every direction. In the centre was a fire which glowed with intense heat, and within the fire, Ezekiel saw four cherubim, strange winged creatures which shot through the sky at lightning speed.

Then Ezekiel saw the four creatures moving on the ground, each with two crystal wheels, full of eyes, trailing fire. The sound of their wings was as loud as a marching army or the roar of rushing water.

As Ezekiel watched, he heard a voice. The creatures lowered their wings and above a sapphire throne, Ezekiel saw something like the shape of a man. He glowed with brilliant fiery light, and shone with all the colours of the rainbow. Ezekiel fell to the ground.

'Stand and I will speak to you,' said the voice. 'I have chosen you to speak to my rebellious people. Don't be afraid, even though they will not want to hear it. Open your mouth and eat what I shall give you.'

Ezekiel opened his mouth, and God gave him a scroll to eat, on which was written many words. It tasted as sweet as honey.

'Go now and speak to my people, and I will help you, even when they refuse to listen,' said God.

223 EZEKIEL'S OBEDIENCE

God spoke through Ezekiel by letting him act out his message. The people watched the prophet and understood by his actions the message that God had for them.

Ezekiel drew a picture of Jerusalem on a clay brick. Then he made armies, battering rams and ramps, and acted out an attack. He ate only wheat and barley, beans and lentils, millet and spelt; he drank only water, and rationed all of it, day after day, so that he became thin and weak.

The people understood that Jerusalem was being besieged by their enemies.

Ezekiel shaved off his hair and beard and divided it into three piles. He took a third of the hair and burned it inside a model of the city of Jerusalem; he took another third and chopped it up around the outside of the model with his sword; the rest, apart from a few strands of hair, he scattered to the wind. Then Ezekiel tucked the few strands carefully inside his cloak.

God's message was clear: many of his people would die by fire or the sword in the siege of Jerusalem; others would be taken into exile and scattered. There would still be a few, a remnant, who would survive and these few would one day return safely to their home in Jerusalem.

224 DRY BONES

Ezekiel spoke to the people through the events in his life for many years.

God's Spirit took Ezekiel to the middle of a valley where, scattered all around him, were human bones, dry and lifeless.

'Speak to these bones!' said God.

So Ezekiel spoke to them with the words God gave him.

'Dry bones, hear the word of the Lord! God says that he will put you together again and cover you with flesh. He will give you breath so that you will once more breathe and have life. Then you will know that he is God.'

A rattling sound echoed through the valley, and one by one the bones moved and locked together, to form skeletons. Slowly the bones were held together with muscles and tendons, and were covered with flesh and wrapped in new skin.

'Tell the wind to give these bodies breath!' said God.

Ezekiel spoke to the wind, and the lungs of the lifeless bodies filled so that they could breathe again and come to life. They stood up and were so many that they formed a large army.

'This is what I will do for my people,' God told Ezekiel. 'I will breathe new life into them. I will take them back to the land of Israel, the land I promised would be their home. Then everyone will know that I am God.'

225 THE EXILES RETURN

The Jewish exiles had been living under the rule of the Persians since they had overthrown the Babylonians. It was time for God's promises to come true.

The messages for his people, spoken by Isaiah, Jeremiah and Ezekiel, were about to take place.

Cyrus, the king of Persia, issued a decree.

'I know that the Lord has put me in charge of many nations. He has told me to rebuild the temple in Jerusalem. Any of you who wishes to return to Jerusalem may now go and help with this work. Those who want to stay here can help in other ways, by making donations of gold or silver or livestock.'

God's people could hardly believe what was happening. After all the years of suffering, living in a foreign land, they were being allowed to go home and instructed to rebuild God's temple.

Preparations were made. Silver and gold were collected. The first group of excited people, led by Zerubbabel, prepared to leave.

'I will give back to you all the things Nebuchadnezzar took from your temple,' said King Cyrus. 'They don't belong here.'

So God's people took back with them not only the riches they had been given, but also 5400 pieces of gold and silver in bowls and dishes and pans.

Over 50,000 people made the journey to Jerusalem along with horses and mules, camels and donkeys.

226 THE REBUILDING BEGINS

When God's people reached their land, they went first to the places that had been their homes. They stayed there for a few months before meeting together in Jerusalem.

There they made plans for the rebuilding of the temple, and Joshua and Zerubbabel started to rebuild the altar and offer sacrifices to God. They celebrated the festivals as they had before they were captured. They worshipped God even before the foundation of the temple was laid. They ordered logs from Tyre and Sidon, as Solomon had before them. They paid masons and carpenters to build the foundations, and when they were restored, the people met together to praise and thank God.

'God is good!' they sang. 'His love and goodness last for ever!'

The people of Samaria and others living in the land of Judah were not happy. In the years that followed, they wrote letters full of lies to the kings ruling at the time. After the death of King Cyrus, they questioned whether the Jews had any right to be there at all and stopped the work of rebuilding.

God spoke through the prophets, Haggai and Zechariah, to encourage the people.

'Keep on building!' they said. 'This is God's will for his people. Do not give up and he will bless us. Jerusalem will once more be a place where God is worshipped.'

King Darius of Persia supported them against their enemies.

'Do not stop the rebuilding work,' ordered King Darius. Then he warned their enemies that if they interfered any more, they would be punished. So the people continued to build the temple until it was finished.

227 ESTHER IS MADE QUEEN

When Xerxes had been king in Persia for three years, he prepared a wonderful banquet in Susa to which everyone important in the land was invited. When everyone was merry and enjoying themselves, Xerxes sent for his wife, Vashti, so he could show off her beauty, but Vashti refused to come.

Xerxes was humiliated in front of his guests. He was so angry that he decided never to see Vashti again and instead sent to every province in his kingdom to find himself a new wife. He ordered that all the most beautiful women should come and take a year of beauty treatments, after which he would choose one of them to be his queen.

Esther was one of the women chosen. Esther, who was very beautiful, was descended from the Jewish captives who had been taken from Jerusalem by the Babylonians. Her uncle Mordecai had looked after her when both her parents died.

'Don't tell them that you are Jewish,' her uncle Mordecai warned when Esther was taken to the palace.

When Xerxes saw Esther, he loved her more than all the other beautiful women. He chose her to be his queen.

228 A PLOT AGAINST KING XERXES

Mordecai worked as a palace official. One day he overheard two of King Xerxes' officers planning an attempt on the king's life.

Mordecai told Esther what he had heard, and Esther told the king. The two officers were executed and the incident was written down in Xerxes' palace records.

Some time later, King Xerxes chose to give great powers to a man called Haman. The king ordered everyone to bow down to Haman and pay him respect. Everyone did this except Mordecai.

The king's attendants tried to persuade Mordecai to bow down, but he would not as he was Jewish, one of God's people.

When Haman realised what was happening, he was very angry. He hated Mordecai. He wanted revenge not just against him, but against all the Jewish people, for he knew that they loved God. So he went to the king with a plot of his own.

'Your majesty,' said Haman, 'there is a people scattered throughout your kingdom who have different customs from us and do not obey your laws. I think you should issue a decree ordering that every one of them be destroyed. I will personally reward the men who carry out the decree.'

'Keep your money,' said King Xerxes. 'Do what you like with these people.'

So the matter was agreed, and a date confirmed for the deaths of every Jewish man, woman and child. The decree was posted up in Susa, and all the people wondered how such a terrible thing could happen.

229 ESTHER PRAYS FOR GUIDANCE

Mordecai put on sackcloth and ashes when he heard about the decree. Jewish people all over the kingdom were doing the same.

Mordecai sent a message to Esther, asking her to beg the king for mercy.

'I cannot go to the king unless he sends for me,' Esther replied. 'Anyone who breaks this rule is put to death.'

'Even a queen will not escape this decree. Perhaps God has made you queen in Persia so that you can save your people.'

'Pray and fast for me,' replied Esther. 'I will do the same. Then I will go to the king, even if I die because of it.'

The next day, Esther went to see the king. When he saw her, he was pleased she had come and was happy to talk to her.

'What can I do for you, Queen Esther?' he asked. 'Ask anything. I will give you half my kingdom.'

'I have prepared a banquet for you and Haman. Please come,' she said.

The king agreed. When Haman received his invitation, he was delighted. When he walked past Mordecai, who did not bow, Haman burned with anger.

'Build a gallows and ask the king to hang Mordecai on it tomorrow!' suggested his friends. So Haman ordered the gallows to be built. After that, he felt much happier.

230 GOD'S ANSWER TO PRAYER

That night, King Xerxes could not sleep.

'Read me the history of my reign,' he said to one of his attendants.

The man read. When he came to the part where Mordecai had saved the king from the plot against his life, King Xerxes stopped his attendant with a question.

'How was Mordecai rewarded?' asked the king.

'He wasn't,' said the attendant. 'There is no mention of it here.'

'Who is in the court at the moment?' Xerxes asked.

Only Haman was there. He had arrived early to ask the king to agree to Mordecai's hanging.

'What do you think is a suitable reward for someone the king wishes to honour?' Xerxes asked Haman.

'Dress him in the king's robe,' said Haman. 'Let him ride one of the king's horses through the streets.'

'Excellent!' said the king. 'Please do all this for Mordecai today.'

Haman felt sick. He obeyed the king, but as soon as he could, he rushed home to tell his wife and friends what had happened.

'This must put you in great danger,' they said. 'You cannot plot against someone whom the king has honoured!'

It was too late. It was time for Esther's banquet.

231 DEATH ON THE GALLOWS

'Well, my queen,' Xerxes said to Esther as the banquet began. 'What would like me to give you? Ask for whatever you wish.'

'Your majesty,' said Esther. 'Please save my life and the lives of all my people! There is a man who has plotted their destruction and we are all to be killed. Our lives hang in the balance.'

'Who is this man? Who wants to destroy your people?' demanded the king.

'This man! This vile Haman!' said Esther, pointing at him.

Haman was terrified. The king and queen stared at him in their anger. Xerxes stormed out of the palace in a rage while Haman begged the queen for mercy. King Xerxes had already made up his mind.

'Haman has built a gallows on which to hang Mordecai,' said a servant.

'Take him! Hang him on his own gallows!' said the king. 'Get him out of my sight!' Haman was dragged from the room.

Then King Xerxes spoke to Esther.

'I cannot undo Haman's decree, for the law cannot be changed, but I can help the Jews fight their enemies and defend themselves,' he said.

Xerxes gave to Mordecai all the power that he had once given to Haman. He put a ring on his finger as a sign of his authority and a gold crown on his head. Mordecai left the palace wearing clothes of blue and white and a purple linen robe.

The Jews were safe. Every year after that they met to remember how Queen Esther had saved them and to celebrate.

232 THE PATIENCE OF JOB

Job had a happy family and many servants. He owned thousands of sheep and camels, and hundreds of cows and donkeys.

Job was rich and he was also a good man. He loved God and did all he could to obey him and live honestly.

One day Satan came to speak to God. Satan was God's enemy.

'Where have you been?' asked God.

'Roaming the earth,' replied Satan. 'Going here and there.'

'Have you seen Job?' asked God. 'He is a truly good man.'

'Of course he's good,' sneered Satan. 'You make it easy for him. He has all he wants. If it were all to be taken away, no doubt he would not love you. He'd be as bad as the next man.'

'We will see,' said God. 'Take away all he loves, but do not harm him.'

Satan caused lightning to fall from the sky and burn up Job's sheep and servants. Raiders carried off Job's camels, and a whirlwind caused the roof to fall in on Job's children and kill them.

'I had nothing when I was born and I shall take nothing with me to my grave. The Lord gave me all that I had and now he has taken it away. Praise the name of God!'

'Job still has his health and strength. He would soon curse you if he was in pain!' said Satan to God.

'We will see,' said God. 'You may take away his health but don't let him die.'

Satan caused Job to be covered all over with painful sores.

'Curse God and die!' urged his wife. 'You cannot still love him!'

'No,' replied Job. 'We were happy to accept the good things that God gave us; we must also accept suffering when it comes.'

233 GOD ANSWERS JOB

When Job's friends heard what had happened, they felt very sorry for him. They had never seen him in such a bad state.

'Why was I born?' Job asked after some days. 'The worst that could have happened has now happened!'

'Perhaps God is punishing you for some terrible sin,' said the first friend. 'Confess your sin and God may make you well.'

'I can think of no such sin,' said Job.

'Well that must be it!' said his second friend. 'You cannot admit you have done something wrong!'

'I will ask God to tell me what I have done wrong,' replied Job.

'Maybe your sin is so huge God will make you suffer even more,' said the third friend.

'You are no help to me at all!' said Job to his friends, and he prayed again in the hope that God would answer him.

'You want to know why you are suffering? Let me ask you some questions. Where were you when I made the world? Have you ever called the morning into being or formed the stars into constellations? Have you given strength to a horse, taught the hawk to fly or the eagle where to build his nest? You have asked me questions, but do you think you can understand the answers?'

Job realised how great and marvellous God was. He did not need to know why he was suffering. He knew that he could trust God whatever happened.

'I am sorry,' replied Job. 'There are things which are too wonderful for me to know.'

'Your friends were wrong,' said God. 'You did not suffer because you sinned. They must ask you to forgive them.'

Job forgave his friends. Then God blessed Job even more than he had before and Job enjoyed a long and happy life.

234 EZRA RETURNS TO JERUSALEM

More than 60 years had passed since the first group of exiles had returned to Jerusalem to rebuild the temple. Now another group followed, with Ezra the priest as their leader.

King Artaxerxes of Persia had given Ezra permission to return.

'Return to Jerusalem with anyone who wants to go. Take a copy of God's law, and my treasurers will give you what you need. You must teach the people God's laws and report back to me,' he wrote.

Ezra was amazed. He called the people to get ready.

'I have told the king that God will protect us on our journey,' he said. 'We must fast and pray before we go and ask God to help us.'

They journeyed safely to Jerusalem and met the others who had returned. Then some of the leaders came to Ezra, embarrassed.

'Since we have returned, some of our people have married wives who do not believe in the living God.'

'What?' cried Ezra, tearing his clothes. He fell on his knees. 'After all God has done for us in bringing us back here?' Then Ezra wept and prayed to God for the forgiveness of all the people.

'I am so sorry, Lord,' he prayed. 'We are your people and we should know the laws you have taught us, but we never learn. We make the same mistakes again and again. Please forgive us.'

Some of the people heard Ezra's prayer. They knew he was right. A large group of men, women and children joined him and wept and prayed with him.

'We have sinned,' they said. 'Forgive us and show us how we can obey you.'

235 NEHEMIAH'S PRAYER

Nehemiah was still in exile, working as cup bearer to King Artaxerxes.

One day he heard news from his brother, Hanani, that the walls of Jerusalem were still in ruins. Nehemiah wept in sorrow and could not eat.

'Lord God, please listen to my prayer,' he said. 'I know that we, your people, have disobeyed you. I am sorry for all the wrong things we have done. I know that we were taken into exile because of our disobedience, but you also promised to return to Jerusalem those people who were obedient. Please let me go back to Jerusalem to help rebuild the walls.'

Four months passed. Then, as Nehemiah was serving the king one day, Artaxerxes noticed that something was wrong.

'Why do you look so sad, Nehemiah?' asked Artaxerxes.

Nehemiah knew that God was answering his prayer.

'The walls surrounding the place where my ancestors are buried need to be rebuilt. I cannot help but be sad,' he said. 'Please let me go to Jerusalem.'

'When will you get back?' replied the king. 'How long will you be away?'

Nehemiah saw that the king had agreed to let him go and that God was on his side. He named a time.

'If you agree to let me go, please provide me with protection for my journey and the materials to rebuild the city gates and walls.'

God answered Nehemiah's prayer. Artaxerxes agreed to everything.

236 REPAIRING THE CITY WALLS

Nehemiah arrived safely in Jerusalem and inspected the walls by night. All that remained were piles of rubble where there should be walls, and the gates were burned.

The next day he went to the city officials and told them his plans, and how King Artaxerxes had given him permission to rebuild the walls.

The people started work straight away. They organised themselves into groups, each working on different sections of the wall. But two men, Sanballat and Tobiah, did not want God's people to succeed. They laughed and made fun of them.

'If a fox walked along the top of that wall, the whole thing would collapse!' they mocked. Then they tried to raise an army.

Nehemiah kept on praying that God would help them. He told the workers to take weapons with them so they were prepared to defend themselves while working. Even when Sanballat and Tobiah plotted to kill him, Nehemiah went on praying.

When the walls were completed, and the new gates were hung, all the people met together. The walls of Jerusalem had been rebuilt in 52 days. Even their enemies knew that God was with them and had made this happen, and they began to be afraid.

237 NEHEMIAH AND THE POOR

Some of the returned exiles were very wealthy. Others were poor. The wealthy lent large sums of money to the poor, but when the poor could not repay their debts, the wealthy men took away their fields. The poor people came to Nehemiah and told him of their needs and of the injustice practised by their fellow Jews.

'Once our fields have gone we have no way of making any money,' cried the people to Nehemiah. 'Then we are forced to sell our children into slavery.'

When Nehemiah heard this, he was very angry. He called the people together.

'What you are doing is against God's law,' he cried. 'We are all members of the same family. We shouldn't be hurting one another. What will our enemies say? Give back everything which does not belong to you.'

The people listened to Nehemiah. He was right. He was their leader, and they respected him. He worked as hard as any of them, and always used his position for the good of the people.

238 EZRA READS GOD'S LAW TO THE PEOPLE

Once the walls were finished, Nehemiah called everyone together.

Ezra climbed a high wooden platform in the square before the water gate, carrying scrolls in his hands. He was a good teacher and knew God's law well. Now he read the scrolls to the people. Everyone listened. One by one, the people understood how disobedient they had been, and began to weep.

'Do not cry,' said Nehemiah. 'Today is a special day. Today we must be happy that we have heard and understood God's law. Go and have something good to eat and drink, and share what you have with each other.'

Day after day the people listened to Ezra as he read God's law. They remembered how God had looked after his people since they first left Egypt. They saw their disobedience.

'We are sorry for all the things our ancestors did to make you angry,' they said to God.

'We are sorry for all our sins.'

239 SINGING NEW SONGS

When it was time to dedicate Jerusalem's new walls to God, the people came together with harps. Nehemiah gave instructions for the singers to form two choirs. Each choir processed around the top of the wall in opposite directions, while the people followed.

The people had wept in Babylon and been too sad to sing to God. Now they sang some new songs.

'Praise the Lord! I will praise the Lord all my life; I will sing to God for as long as I live!

'How happy are the people who trust God, the maker of heaven and earth, the sea and all that lives in them. How happy are the people who know that God will help them.

'God cares for the oppressed, and gives food to the hungry. God sets free the prisoners and gives sight to the blind. God looks after those who are strangers in foreign lands and those who have lost parents, wives or husbands.

'Our God reigns for ever! Praise the Lord!'

They met together in God's temple. Every man, woman and child sang to God and was happy. They knew God had kept his promises.

'The Lord builds up Jerusalem; he gathers up the exiles and returns them to Israel,' they sang. 'He heals the broken hearted and binds up their wounds.

'Our Lord is great and mighty; his understanding is without limit. Sing to the Lord with thanksgiving! Make music to our God upon the harp! The Lord loves those who look to him for help, who put their trust in his unfailing love.

'Praise the Lord! Praise the Lord!'

Some time later, Nehemiah returned to work for King Artaxerxes, as he had agreed to do.

240 PREPARING THE WAY

When Nehemiah left Jerusalem, God's people began to rebuild their lives. For a while they remembered how they had hated their time in exile and how much they wanted to come home.

Time passed. Sometimes their lives were a struggle. Things were not always as easy as they had hoped.

'People who don't worship God seem to live happily,' they said. 'Is there any point in keeping God's laws?'

Malachi brought God's words to his people.

'"I love you, just as I have always loved you from the beginning. Remember how a child obeys his father. Think about how a servant respects his master. I am your father; I am your master."

'The priests have stopped obeying the laws God gave them. You marry wives from the people who worship false gods. You don't keep the sabbath or trust God to provide for your needs.

'One day God will come to live among you! Look out for his messenger. The one who comes will come to judge and to save. He will be like a fire which makes gold pure and silver without impurities. People who do what is right will be happy on that day!'

Nehemiah returned again to Jerusalem and tried to put right the things which God had warned the people about through Malachi. After Malachi, there were no more prophets in the land for 400 years.

THE NEW TESTAMENT

241 THE ANGEL IN THE TEMPLE

Zechariah was a priest living in the hill country of Judea. He and his wife Elizabeth had loved and served God all their lives. God had not blessed them with children.

Now Zechariah had been chosen to burn the incense in the temple—a rare honour as there were many priests, and they were chosen to do this by lot. Outside the temple, in the morning sunshine, people were praying. Inside the temple, where it was cool and quiet, Zechariah lit the incense.

Then Zechariah realised he was not alone. Standing on the right hand side of the altar was an angel.

'Don't be afraid,' said the angel. It was clear that Zechariah was terrified. 'God has heard your prayers. Elizabeth will have a son called John, and God's Holy Spirit will be with him in a special way. He will help people understand what God wants of them, so that they will be ready for him.'

'Can this be true?' asked Zechariah. 'Surely Elizabeth is now too old to have children.'

'My name is Gabriel,' said the angel, 'and I stand in the presence of God. Because you question the truth of the message I have brought to you from God, you will not be able to speak until everything I have told you has come true.'

Zechariah had been in the temple for longer than was usual. The people outside began to wonder what had happened. When Zechariah came out, he tried to tell them about the angel, but he could not speak. He waved his arms about. The people could not understand him but they realised he must have had some sort of vision.

Some time later, Elizabeth found she was expecting a baby...

242 ANOTHER VISIT FROM GABRIEL

The angel Gabriel had another surprise announcement to make.

He went to see Mary, who lived in Nazareth in Galilee. Mary was not much more than a girl but she was engaged to be married to Joseph, the local carpenter. They did not yet live together as man and wife.

'Mary,' said Gabriel. 'God is with you!'

Mary was afraid. She didn't know what to think.

'There is no need to be afraid!' said Gabriel. 'You are going to have a baby, and you are to call him Jesus. He will be known as God's son and will be a king who will reign for ever!'

'I am not yet married,' said Mary. 'How can I have a baby?'

'The Holy Spirit will make this happen, for God is able to do anything. Another woman in your family, Elizabeth, is now six months pregnant. Everyone said that she couldn't have children, but with God, nothing is impossible.'

'I will do anything God wants me to,' said Mary. 'I am ready to serve him in any way he chooses.'

Then Gabriel left Mary.

243 TWO SPECIAL BABIES

Mary thought about what the angel had told her. If Elizabeth was expecting a baby, perhaps Mary should go and visit her and talk to her about what had happened. Elizabeth lived in the hills. Mary prepared for her journey and went to stay with her.

When she reached Zechariah's house, Mary embraced Elizabeth. Then the baby inside Elizabeth's belly jumped with joy.

'God has blessed you!' Elizabeth told Mary. 'And he will bless your baby too. You have been willing to do what God has asked of you, and you will be rewarded. Why am I so lucky to have you come to stay with me?'

'God is very great!' said Mary. 'I am no one, yet God has made me special by giving me this amazing thing to do. He has always been good to people who try to listen to him and follow his ways. He was good to Abraham and Isaac and Jacob and is good to us now. God always chooses people who feel they have nothing to offer, and he makes them great. He also sends away people who think they are too good or important to need his help. God is good.'

Mary stayed in the hills with Elizabeth for three months before returning to her home in Nazareth.

244 ZECHARIAH SPEAKS AGAIN

Nine months had passed since Zechariah had seen the angel Gabriel in the temple. Now Elizabeth was ready to give birth to her baby. It was a little boy, just as Gabriel had told her. Elizabeth was overjoyed, and her friends and neighbours shared in her happiness.

Eight days later, the baby boy was circumcised. They were ready to call him Zechariah after his father, but Elizabeth insisted he should be called John.

'What does Zechariah say?' they said. Then Zechariah asked for a writing tablet so he could tell them. He had not spoken since he met the angel.

'His name is John,' he wrote.

As soon as he had finished writing, he was able to speak once more. The first words he spoke were in praise of God who had blessed them with this special child.

Everyone was amazed. They couldn't stop talking about these strange events.

'God has not forgotten us, his people,' Zechariah said. 'He is sending his chosen one to save us from our enemies. And he has chosen this child, my child John, to be the one who will prepare the way and tell us about the one who is to come, and to lead us into the way of peace.'

245 JOSEPH, THE CARPENTER

Mary was happy to serve God and do all that he wanted of her.
Joseph was rather sad. He knew that Mary's baby was not his baby, but
he cared about Mary. He did not want her to face bringing up her baby
alone. He didn't want people to be unkind to her. Should he marry her
as they had planned?

Then one night Joseph dreamed a strange dream in which an angel
appeared to him.

'You need not worry about marrying Mary,' the angel said. 'The Holy
Spirit has caused the baby to grow inside her. She will have a baby
boy and you must call him Jesus, because he will be the Saviour of the
world.'

Joseph needed no further reassurance to marry Mary. He did what
the angel of the Lord had told him.

246 THE ROMAN CENSUS

The months passed quickly and soon the time came for Mary's baby to be born. It looked as though this would not happen in Nazareth, but in Bethlehem.

The Roman emperor, Caesar Augustus, wanted to tax his people. He ordered a census so that everyone had to go to the town of their ancestors to be counted. This meant that Joseph had to take Mary with him to Bethlehem, because he belonged to the family of King David.

Mary and Joseph made their way to the village of Bethlehem in Judea.

The roads were full of people travelling, all obeying the commands of their Roman ruler.

247 THE BABY BORN IN BETHLEHEM

Bethlehem was bustling with people.

Men, women and children had all come to be registered there. By the time Mary and Joseph arrived, it was already difficult to find somewhere to stay.

Mary felt tired and weary. She was starting to feel the pains that meant her baby would soon be born.

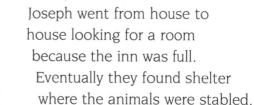

Joseph went from house to house looking for a room because the inn was full. Eventually they found shelter where the animals were stabled. That night, Mary gave birth to a baby boy, her firstborn child. She wrapped him in strips of cloth and made a bed for him in a manger, because there was no room anywhere else.

248 SHEPHERDS HEAR GOOD NEWS

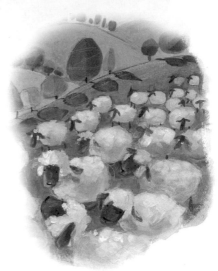

While Jesus was being cradled by his mother Mary, shepherds were on the hills outside Bethlehem, looking after their flocks of sheep.

The soft flickering flames suddenly gave way to dazzling light as an angel appeared in the night sky. The shepherds were terrified.

'Don't be afraid!' said the angel. 'I have come with good news. Tonight, in Bethlehem, a baby has been born who is the Saviour of the world. You will find him wrapped in strips of cloth, lying in a manger.'

Then the sound of hundreds of angels, singing and praising God, filled their ears.

'Glory to God in the highest heaven!' the angels sang. 'And peace on earth.'

The shepherds wasted no time. They ran down the hillside, determined to find the baby who had been born that night.

They found the place where Mary and Joseph were staying and knew that this baby, lying in the manger, was the baby the angel had told them about.

They went from there to tell everyone what they had seen and heard, so that no one could be in any doubt about who the baby was. Mary, watching Jesus sleeping, thought about all she had heard that night.

249 THE LONG-AWAITED SAVIOUR

When Jesus was just over a month old, Mary and Joseph prepared to take him to the temple in Jerusalem. They went to thank God for his safe birth and offer a sacrifice of two pigeons.

As they went into the temple courts, they met there a man called Simeon. Simeon had been waiting for the day when God would send his Messiah, the chosen one who would save his people. He believed that God had promised him that he would see this Saviour before he died.

When Simeon saw Mary and Joseph and the baby boy in their arms, he knew that the special day had arrived. He took Jesus from them and praised God.

'Lord, you can let me now die in peace, because I have seen with my own eyes the Saviour you have promised your people. This child will reveal your truth to all people on earth and be everything the people have been waiting for.'

Mary and Joseph listened in some surprise to his words but before they had taken it all in, an elderly woman approached them. Anna was a prophetess who had lived in the temple, praying and worshipping God for most of her long life. She also knew that Jesus was God's chosen one, and she thanked God for him.

Mary and Joseph made their offering. They wondered at all they had learned that day about their baby son.

250 WISE MEN FROM THE EAST

Wise men living in the east had been studying the night skies when Jesus was born. They saw a strange new star and wondered what it could mean.

They set out on a journey, following the star, because they thought it heralded the birth of a new king, and they wanted to worship him.

When they reached Jerusalem, they stopped at King Herod's palace.

'Where is the child born to be king of the Jewish people?' they asked. 'We have come to pay our respects, to welcome and worship him.'

Herod was disturbed by their arrival. What king could there be apart from him? Quickly, Herod consulted the chief priests and teachers of the law. They told him what they knew from the ancient prophecies: the king would be born in Bethlehem.

Herod then talked to his eastern visitors and tried to find out exactly when they had first seen the star. This way he could know how old the baby might be.

Then he sent them to Bethlehem.

'If you find the king,' he said, craftily, 'let me know. I would like to be able to worship him as well.'

251 GOLD, FRANKINCENSE AND MYRRH

The wise men continued their journey until they reached Bethlehem, where the star seemed to stop over a house. They went inside and found Mary with her young child.

The wise men knew they had found the right place and worshipped Jesus, the new king. Then they gave him the gifts they had brought: gold, frankincense and myrrh.

They stopped for the night before beginning their return journey, but they did not go back the way they had come. In the night they had dreamed that it was not safe to return to King Herod.

252 THE JOURNEY TO EGYPT

After the wise men had left, Joseph also had a strange dream. In it, he was warned by an angel.

'Wake up!' said the angel. 'Herod plans to kill Jesus. You must take your family and escape to Egypt.'

It was still night when Joseph woke Mary and took her and her child to safety.

Meanwhile Herod waited for the wise men to return. A day passed. Two days passed. Soon he realised that he had been tricked. The men from the east were not going to return. He was furious. Herod was a cruel man. He thought of another way to get rid of Jesus. He had worked out how old Jesus must be from what the wise men had told him and so he gave orders to kill all boys under two years old in the area.

Herod did not know that Jesus was safely in Egypt. Joseph kept him there until Herod had died.

Then, when Jesus was a little boy, another angel came to Joseph in a dream and told him it was safe to return. Joseph travelled to Nazareth and they made their home there. Jesus grew up strong and healthy and wise.

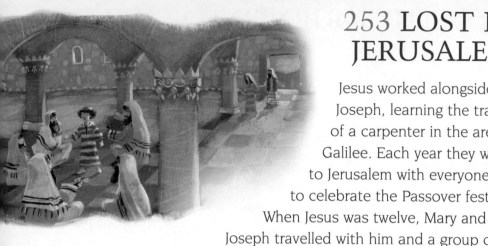

253 LOST IN JERUSALEM

Jesus worked alongside Joseph, learning the trade of a carpenter in the area of Galilee. Each year they went to Jerusalem with everyone else to celebrate the Passover festival. When Jesus was twelve, Mary and Joseph travelled with him and a group of other people from Nazareth. At the end of the festival, they went home.

Mary and Joseph had been walking for some time when they realised that Jesus was missing. They had assumed he was walking with friends. They began to panic. Where could he be?

They returned to Jerusalem and questioned the market traders but at the end of three days, Mary was desperate.

Then they went to the temple. Surrounded by experts and teachers of the law, there was Mary's son. Jesus was listening to the teachers and asking questions. Mary watched as he spoke and saw that his elders were surprised by his answers.

'Where have you been?' she asked. 'We have been so worried! We have been searching everywhere for you.'

'I have been here in my Father's house,' Jesus replied. 'Did you not guess?'

Jesus was a good son. He went back home with them. As he grew older, Mary remembered all the special things that had happened to him.

254 JOHN THE BAPTIST

Jesus was not the only boy to have grown up. Elizabeth's son, John, had not only become a man, he had gone to live alone in the desert.

When he was ready, John started to do the work he knew God wanted him to do. He started to tell people how God wanted them to live. He was not a well-dressed man; in fact, he looked rather wild. He wore clothes of camel's hair and ate strange food. People listened to him. Somehow they knew that what he said was true. They knew that God spoke through him and they needed to do the things he said.

'Stop doing things that are wrong. Obey God,' John told them. 'Be baptised, and show that you are sorry and that God has forgiven you.'

The people came to the River Jordan and John baptised them.

'It is not enough that Abraham is your ancestor,' he said. 'You must show that you love God by the way you live. If you have two tunics, give one away to someone in need. If you have plenty of food, share it with someone who has nothing. If you are a tax collector, live honestly and fairly. Don't cheat people. If you are a soldier, don't bully people.'

'Who is this man?' the people whispered. 'Is John God's Saviour?'

John heard them.

'I baptise you with water,' he said. 'Soon someone will come who will baptise you with God's own Spirit!'

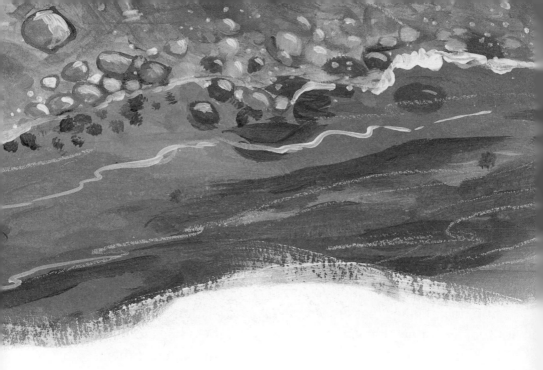

255 JESUS IS BAPTISED

Jesus came to the River Jordan one day. He was now a man of about 30 and had been a carpenter for many years.

Jesus stepped forward as John was calling people to be baptised.

John knew straight away who Jesus was. He also knew he was not worthy to baptise Jesus!

Jesus persuaded him. He told John it was what God wanted. As Jesus came out of the water, God's Spirit came down from heaven like a dove and rested on Jesus. A voice from heaven said:

'You are my son. I love you very much. I am pleased with you.'

256 JESUS IS TESTED

After his baptism, Jesus was led by God's Spirit into the desert. He went without food for 40 days and at the end of this time, Jesus was weak and very hungry.

God's enemy, the devil, tried to test Jesus.

'You need food,' he said. 'If you are God's son, you can make this stone turn into bread.'

'Life is more than just food,' replied Jesus, quoting God's law.

Then the devil led Jesus to a very high place and showed him all the kingdoms of the world.

'Look at all this!' whispered the devil. 'I will give it to you, if you bow down and worship me.'

'God has said that we must worship him alone,' replied Jesus.

Then the devil took Jesus to Jerusalem. They stood on the highest part of the temple.

'God has promised to send his angels to protect you,' continued the devil. 'Throw yourself off the temple so we can see his power!'

'God's law says that we must not put him to the test,' Jesus replied.

The devil had tried to tempt Jesus to break God's laws and do something wrong, but Jesus would not give in. The devil left, and Jesus was alone.

257 THE FOUR FISHERMEN

Jesus returned to Galilee and began to travel around, telling the people the good news of salvation.

'Stop doing things that are wrong; live your lives the way God wants you to. Love God and learn to love the people around you as much as you love yourself.'

Jesus watched Peter and Andrew casting their nets into the waters of Lake Galilee.

'Come and follow me!' Jesus said to the two brothers. 'You can catch people for God instead of fish.'

Peter and Andrew dropped their nets and joined Jesus straight away.

Further along the lakeside, they saw James and his brother John mending their nets. Their father Zebedee was in the boat with them.

'Come and follow me!' called Jesus.

James and John got out of the boat and went with him.

These four fishermen became Jesus' first disciples. Jesus went with them to their homes in Capernaum. There Jesus taught in the synagogue. Crowds of people came to him for help and he healed those who were ill.

258 THE BEST WINE OF ALL

One day, there was a wedding in the village of Cana. Jesus' mother, Mary, had been invited. Jesus and some of his disciples went too.

While everyone was celebrating and enjoying themselves, the wine ran out. Mary went to Jesus and told him what had happened.

'It is not yet the right time for me,' Jesus replied.

Mary knew her son was special. She knew he would help in some way.

'Do whatever he asks,' she whispered to the servants.

'Fill these six jars with water,' Jesus said. The jars were used for washing; they were very large, each holding many gallons of water.

The servants filled them with water and when they had finished, Jesus asked them to pour some out and offer it to the man in charge of the feast. The servants were anxious, but when they poured it, they saw that the water had become wine.

The man tasted it and then went to speak to the bridegroom.

'This wine is wonderful,' he said. 'Most people serve the cheap wine last when no one notices, but you have saved the best until the end.'

The disciples saw what Jesus had done and were amazed. They began to realise that he was no ordinary man.

259 THE GOOD NEWS

Many people throughout Galilee had seen the way Jesus healed people and had heard him talk about the way God loved and cared for everyone.

It was time for Jesus to visit Nazareth, his home town. He went as usual to the synagogue on the sabbath day and stood up, ready to read from the scriptures. Someone handed him the scroll, containing the words of the prophet Isaiah.

'God's Spirit is on me,' read Jesus. 'He has chosen me to bring good news to the poor, to free those who are in chains, to give sight to the blind, to help those who are suffering and to tell everyone that God's blessing has come.' Jesus rolled up the scroll and sat down. 'That was written hundreds of years ago. Today, here, you have seen it come true.'

The people stared at him. They began to whisper among themselves.

'This is Joseph's boy,' they said. 'He's no one special.'

'I know what you think. And because you cannot believe, you will see no miracles here,' replied Jesus.

The people of Nazareth were angry. They would not let Jesus stay in the town, but drove him away.

260 THE MAN ON THE MAT

Jesus received a very different reaction in Capernaum. Crowds of people gathered to hear him speak about God wherever he went.

Four men were particularly keen to find Jesus. They were carrying their friend, who was lying on a mat. They wanted Jesus to heal him because he could not walk.

When they reached the house where Jesus was speaking, they found people were packed all around him and spilling out of the doorway.

Outside the house, steps led up to the roof. The men climbed up, and dug through the mud and branches that made up the roof until there was a hole large enough to lower the man and his mat down in front of Jesus and the amazed crowd.

Jesus saw how certain the friends were that he could help them. He spoke to the paralysed man.

'Go,' he said, 'your sins are forgiven.'

The Pharisees and other religious experts were shocked. Surely only God could forgive sins? This was too much! Jesus knew what they were thinking.

'Which is easier,' Jesus asked, 'to forgive this man's sins, or to make him walk? Nothing is impossible for God.' Then he looked again at the paralysed man and spoke. 'Stand up, take your mat, and go home.'

The man stood up. His friends were overjoyed. Everyone else was amazed! They praised God for the miracle they had seen.

273

261 MATTHEW JOINS JESUS

Jesus first saw Matthew when he was walking beside Lake Galilee, teaching the crowds of people who followed him.

Matthew was a tax collector and he had set up his booth where he collected money for the Romans day by day.

'Come, follow me,' Jesus said to him.

Matthew stopped what he was doing straight away. He joined the others who were following Jesus and walked with them.

Later that day, Matthew invited Jesus back to his house for dinner with many of his friends.

When the religious leaders saw that Jesus was Matthew's guest, they were shocked and outraged.

'Why does Jesus mix with such terrible people?' they asked the disciples.

Jesus heard them.

'Healthy people don't need a doctor,' he said. 'I am here with the people who most need to hear God's message.'

262 LIVING GOD'S WAY

The people who heard Jesus speak told others about him. Soon there were people following Jesus wherever he went.

One day Jesus walked up the hillside overlooking Lake Galilee. He sat down and began to talk to the people about the way God wanted them to live their lives.

'The people who are happy are not the proud ones who think highly of themselves, but those who know how much they need God's help and forgiveness,' Jesus said. 'If you follow God's ways, you will be like a little salt in the cooking pot, making the whole meal taste good; or like a lamp shining brightly in a dark place, bringing light so that all can see.'

Then Jesus began to talk about God's law. It was the law the Pharisees knew all about, but Jesus spoke about it in a way that no one had understood before.

'If someone hurts you, don't try to get your own back,' said Jesus. 'Instead, be kind to those who hurt you. Go out of your way to help everyone. God's law says that we must love not only those who are our friends, family and neighbours, but also our enemies as well. It's easy to love people who already love us. God wants us to be different. God is perfect. We must try to be like him.'

263 LESSONS ON PRAYER

Jesus went on to teach the people how they should talk to God in prayer.

'Be careful,' said Jesus, 'not to pray with empty meaningless words so that others will notice you. Make sure your prayers are honest conversations between you and God. God sees everything. He knows what you want to tell him before you begin to speak. Talk to God without drawing attention to yourself.'

Then Jesus gave his disciples a pattern to use when they prayed.
'Our Father in heaven,
hallowed be your name,
your kingdom come,
your will be done,
on earth as it is in heaven.
Give us today our daily bread.
And forgive us our sins,
as we also have forgiven those who sin against us.
And lead us not into temptation,
but deliver us from the evil one.

'Begin by speaking to God as your father in heaven,' explained Jesus. 'God is holy, so ask that God's name be treated as holy, and that God's kingdom will arrive quickly. Ask God for the things that you need for today, like bread. Then ask for his forgiveness, and at the same time, forgive anyone who may have hurt you. And ask God for help, to keep you from doing anything wrong.'

264 DON'T WORRY

Jesus looked at the people around him. Some were poor; others were sad or anxious; some could not walk or see.

'Don't worry about the everyday matters of living,' Jesus said. 'Don't worry about what you will eat or drink, or what clothes you're going to wear. Look around you at the wild birds. They don't have huge stores of food. They rely on God to feed them. God cares about them, but he cares about you even more than he cares about the birds. You will not live longer by worrying about your life.

'As for worrying about clothes, look at the lilies that grow in the fields. They do not work or dress themselves, but God has made them beautiful.

'If you put God first, he will make sure that you have everything you need and much more besides.'

265 A STORY ABOUT TWO HOUSES

As people listened to what Jesus had to say, they divided into groups. Many were eager to hear more. They wanted to know how to please God. Some were suspicious or angry at this way of teaching. It was different from the teaching of the scribes and Pharisees. So Jesus told a story.

'If you listen to me and do what I say, you will be like a wise man who built his house on a rock. Before he started work, the man made sure that his house had firm foundations on the rock. Then when the rain battered against the house and the wind blew around it, it did not collapse. It remained firm and solid.

'If you take no notice of what I have said, you will be like a foolish man who built his house on sand. When the wind blew and the rain beat against his house, it had no foundations and so it fell down. The walls and roof, the door and all his belongings were swept away.

'Don't be like the foolish man, regretting his mistake when it was too late to change things. Be like the wise man; listen well and act on what you hear.'

266 JESUS AND THE ROMAN OFFICER

The crowd stayed with Jesus as he walked back to Capernaum, but the people fell back as a Roman centurion rushed towards him.

The centurion was clearly upset.

'Will you help me?' he asked Jesus. 'One of my servants is very ill. He is in terrible pain and cannot move at all.'

'Shall I come to your house?' said Jesus. 'Then I will heal him.'

The centurion stopped Jesus.

'Lord, I don't deserve to have you under my roof. I know that if you just say that my servant is healed, he will be healed. I'm a centurion, and I know about power and authority. Those above me expect me to do what they tell me, while I tell people below me to come and go, and they obey me.'

Jesus was amazed at the centurion's faith.

'I have not found anyone here with such faith,' he said. 'Return to your home, and you will find that your servant is well again.'

The centurion went home. His servant had recovered, just as Jesus had promised he would.

267 THE WIDOW'S ONLY SON

Soon afterwards Jesus and his disciples visited the town of Nain. As they approached the gates of the town, another group of people was making its way to the cemetery on the hillside outside.

Jesus saw that they were carrying the body of a young man on a stretcher. The dead man's mother was weeping as she followed behind; he was her only son, and her husband had already died.

Jesus was moved by the woman's sadness.

'There's no need to cry,' Jesus said. He went up to the stretcher and touched it. The men carrying it stopped and waited.

'Young man,' Jesus said to the dead man, 'sit up!'

As soon as Jesus spoke, the young man stirred and sat up on the stretcher. He began talking straight away! His mother wept with delight at the miracle that had happened. Jesus took him by the hand, and helped him to his mother.

Everyone was amazed and there was much joy among the people. They could hardly believe what they saw. Some among them remembered the stories of Elisha who had lived nearby. He had also brought a boy back from the dead and had restored him to his mother in much the same way.

'Praise God!' they said. After this, the news spread all over the country about what Jesus had done.

268 THE STORY OF THE FARMER AND THE SEED

Jesus went from village to village telling people about how much God loved them and healing people who were ill. When he returned to Galilee, Jesus taught the people using parables—stories about things they understood but with a special meaning.

'A farmer went out to sow some seed,' began Jesus. 'He took handfuls of seed, and cast it from side to side as he walked along.

'Some seed fell on the path. Birds came and gobbled it up. Some fell on stony soil. The seed grew quite quickly but its roots had not stretched deep into the soil; when the sun beat down, the plants shrivelled and died. Some landed among thorns and was choked, so it could not produce fruit. Some seed fell on good rich soil, where it grew until it produced a good harvest.'

Later, when the disciples were alone with Jesus, they asked him what the story about the farmer and the seed meant.

'The farmer who sows the seed is like God planting his message of truth in those who hear it,' Jesus said. 'Some people are like the soil on the path. They hear the message about God, but quickly forget it. Some people are like the stony soil. They try to obey God, but give up when things get difficult or people criticise them for their faith. Some are like the seed that fell among thorns. They try to follow God, but become distracted by money or other worries and their faith is choked.

'Others are like the good rich soil. They hear the word and grow up like strong healthy plants, living fruitful lives that God can use, not being swayed by the cares of the world, and sharing their faith with others.'

269 SECRETS OF GOD'S KINGDOM

Jesus told other stories to explain what God's kingdom is like.

'Imagine that there is some treasure hidden in a field. One day, a man accidentally finds the treasure. He buries it again quickly, then goes back home. He sells his home, his furniture, his cooking pots, even his donkey, so that he can buy the field. Then the treasure is his, and nothing could be worth more than that.'

The people listened. Some of them understood. Jesus meant that God's kingdom was more valuable than anything they owned. It was worth doing anything to be part of it.

Then Jesus told another story.

'God's kingdom is like a man who buys and sells pearls. One day he finds an extremely beautiful pearl which is more valuable than any other. What does the man do? He goes home and sells all his possessions so that he can buy it and have the beautiful pearl for himself.'

270 THE STORM ON THE LAKE

It was evening, and Jesus was tired after teaching the crowds of people all day.

'Let's cross to the other side of the lake,' Jesus said to his friends. So they prepared the boat and set sail.

Jesus went to the stern of the boat and lay down, a cushion under his head. He was soon fast asleep.

At first the boat bobbed up and down gently and rhythmically. Jesus' friends thought about all they had seen and heard during the day as they made progress across Lake Galilee. Then, as so often happened on that stretch of water, the wind suddenly changed direction. The waves began to crash over the side and the boat lurched dangerously up and down.

The men clung to the mast of the boat. Even the fishermen among them knew they were in danger. They felt sure they were going to drown. Jesus was still fast asleep.

'Master, help us!' they shouted, waking him. 'Don't you care if we die?'

Jesus stood up. He spoke to the wind and to the waves.

'Be calm!' he said. The wind dropped and the sea was still.

Then Jesus turned to look at his frightened disciples.

'Why are you afraid?' he asked. 'Don't you trust me?'

Jesus' friends were amazed. They had had no idea he had so much power.

'Who is he?' they asked one another. 'Even the wind and the waves do what he says!'

271 ANOTHER VISIT TO CAPERNAUM

When Jesus arrived in Capernaum, the crowds came to greet him. Jairus, the leader of the synagogue, hurried to speak to Jesus.

'Please help us,' he cried. 'My daughter is dying. She is only twelve years old. Will you come and help her?'

Jesus followed Jairus and they made their way through the crowds but suddenly Jesus stopped.

'Who touched me?' he asked those around him.

As the people in the crowd all denied it, Peter spoke to Jesus.

'Master,' he said, 'there are crowds all around, pressing close to you. Any one of these people could have touched you.'

Then a woman stepped forward, seeing that she could not hide from Jesus. 'It was me,' she said, falling to her knees. 'I have been suffering for many years. No doctor has been able to help me. I thought that if I could only touch the hem of your cloak, it would be enough.'

'There's no need to be afraid any more,' he said. 'Your faith has healed you.'

Just then, someone came from Jairus' house with news.

'Sir,' he said. 'It's too late. Your daughter has died.'

Jesus looked at Jairus. Jairus was close to tears.

'Don't be afraid. Keep on believing; your daughter will be well.'

'Stop crying,' said Jesus to the mourners who were weeping and wailing. 'The little girl isn't dead; she's only asleep.'

Jesus went inside with the girl's father and mother, and with Peter, James and John. Then Jesus took the little girl's hand in his.

'Get up, little girl,' he said.

The girl's eyes opened immediately, and she began to breathe again. Jairus and his wife were astonished and very happy.

272 THE SECRET VISIT

Many people heard about the amazing things Jesus did and the incredible things he said. Among them was Nicodemus, a Pharisee, a member of the important religious council, the Sanhedrin. Nicodemus was eager to hear what Jesus had to say, but he was also afraid. He knew that Jesus was making enemies among the religious leaders.

So Nicodemus visited Jesus at night.

'Teacher,' said Nicodemus, 'I have seen you do amazing things. God is obviously with you.'

Jesus could see that Nicodemus longed to know more about God.

'To see God's kingdom you need to be born again,' said Jesus.

'That's impossible!' said Nicodemus. 'No one can do that.'

'Your mother cannot give birth to you again,' said Jesus. 'But God can give you a completely new start, a new life with God by the power of his Holy Spirit.'

'How can I do this?' asked Nicodemus.

'Believe in the Saviour God has sent into the world. God has love enough for everyone, but people love the darkness rather than light. They want to hide the evil things they do and are afraid that the light will show up their sins. God has sent his son so that all who sin can be forgiven and have eternal life. They need only put their trust in God's son to know that forgiveness.

'Anyone who believes in God's son will not die, but will live for ever!'

273 THE WOMAN WITH FIVE HUSBANDS

Jesus once travelled through a village called Sychar in Samaria on his way back to Galilee.

His friends went to buy food in the village and left him sitting by the well, the well that Jacob had drunk from many generations before. It was midday and the sun beat down on him. Jesus felt tired and thirsty.

Just then a Samaritan woman walked towards him. Although it was the time of day when people would usually be sheltering in the shade, she had brought her jar to fill with water.

'Please will you give me a drink?' asked Jesus.

The woman looked at him.

'You're a Jew, aren't you?' she said. 'And I'm a Samaritan. You know our people are enemies? How can you ask me for a drink?'

'If you knew who I am, you would be asking me for water!' said Jesus. 'I would not give you water from this well, but God's living water, so that you would never be thirsty again.'

'I want that water!' replied the woman. 'It would save me having to come here every day.'

'Go and tell your husband what I have said, and come back,' said Jesus.

'I have no husband,' the woman replied.

'That's true,' said Jesus. 'You have been married five times, and now you live with someone you are not even married to.'

The woman was amazed. How could Jesus know these things about her? She forgot about her water pot and ran to the town.

'Quickly!' she said to as many people as possible. 'Come and meet a very special man. He knows all about me! Could he be the Saviour God has promised to send?'

274 THE END OF JOHN'S WORK

God had chosen John the Baptist to prepare the way for Jesus, to teach people that he was the Saviour God had promised.

John's message was a hard one. By speaking the truth, and telling people to stop doing the things that were against God's laws, he made enemies.

One of the people he had upset was Herodias, the woman married to King Herod. She had been married before to Herod's brother, Philip, and Philip was still alive. This was forbidden by Jewish law.

Herod had put John in prison, but he was afraid to punish him further because he knew he was a man of God, and he knew it would cause a riot among the people.

Then, on his birthday, Herod held a party. Herodias' beautiful daughter got up and danced. Herod was entranced and told her she could ask anything of him, and she could have it.

The girl asked her mother what she should ask for, and Herod regretted his promise immediately. She asked for the head of John the Baptist on a plate.

Herod knew that all his guests had heard his promise. He could not refuse her request. John was executed and his head brought to Herod.

John's work was over. Some of his friends buried his body. Then they made sure Jesus knew what had happened.

Jesus was very sad. He wanted to be alone to think, to grieve and to pray. Wherever he went, people followed him.

275 FIVE ROLLS AND TWO LITTLE FISH

Jesus went by boat into the hills on the far side of Lake Galilee. When he found people waiting for him even there, he could not turn them away. He healed those who were ill until late in the day.

There were more than 5000 men there, plus the women and children. Jesus turned to Philip, who came from nearby Bethsaida.

'Do you know where we could buy bread for all these people?' Jesus asked.

'Even if I did, it would cost far too much!' answered Philip.

Then Andrew, another of Jesus' friends, noticed a boy in the crowd who had with him a picnic lunch of five small barley rolls and two little fish. He brought the boy to Jesus.

'This boy has some food,' he said, 'but it won't go very far!'

'Ask the people to sit down,' he said to his friends.

The people sat down on the grass and watched as Jesus took the food and asked God to bless it. Then he began to break the bread and fish into pieces, and passed it around.

The people shared the food among themselves and ate until they were no longer hungry. Then Jesus' friends went among the people picking up anything that was left over. They collected twelve baskets full of leftover pieces.

Over 5000 people had eaten with Jesus that day.

276 WALKING ON WATER

In the evening Jesus said goodbye to the crowd and told his disciples to go back across the lake without him. Then he went further into the hills to pray. Jesus needed to spend time talking to God, his Father.

It was a windy night and the disciples worked hard, being buffeted against the waves. Just before dawn, they saw a figure out on the water. They didn't realise it was Jesus, and they were alarmed.

'Don't be afraid!' Jesus said to them, as he walked towards them across the water. 'It's me.'

Peter heard Jesus' voice.

'If it's really you,' he shouted, 'tell me to come to you on the water.'

'Come on then,' said Jesus.

Peter stepped out of the boat in the darkness, on to the choppy waves. He walked towards Jesus until a gust of wind blew around him. Then Peter panicked.

'Lord, save me!' he called out to Jesus as he began to sink.

Jesus reached out and took Peter's hand.

'Why didn't you trust me?' he asked, as he helped Peter back into the boat. The wind dropped and the sea became calm.

The other disciples, who had seen it all, knelt before Jesus.

'You really must be God's Son,' they said.

277 THE MAN WHO COULD NOT HEAR

When Jesus was travelling through the region of the Decapolis, a group of people came out to meet him. They brought to him a deaf man who could hardly talk.

'Please help him,' they said. 'Make him well.'

Jesus took the man away from his friends and all those who were there so he could be alone with him. Jesus put his fingers in the man's ears, then put some of his own saliva on the man's tongue. He prayed for the man, asking for God's help.

'Open up!' Jesus said.

The man could hear. The man could talk. Suddenly the man couldn't stop talking! His friends and the others in the crowd were amazed and excited.

Jesus tried to keep them from telling anyone else about it, but they wouldn't listen. They could talk of nothing else except of how Jesus had given speech and hearing to a deaf and mute man.

278 ON THE MOUNTAIN

One day Jesus took his closest friends, Peter, James and John, to a high mountain.

While they were there, something strange happened to Jesus. As they watched, Jesus' face and clothing became like a bright shining light. Then two men appeared, standing beside Jesus and talking to him. They recognised the men as Moses and Elijah.

Peter could not keep quiet.

'Let us build three shelters, one for each of you,' he called out. Before Peter could finish speaking, a bright cloud covered them, and they heard a voice speaking from heaven.

'This is my son,' said the voice. 'I love him. I am pleased with him. Listen to him.'

At the sound of God's voice, Jesus' friends were terrified. They fell to the ground.

While they were lying there, Jesus came and touched them.

'Don't be frightened,' he said. 'And don't tell anyone what you saw until you have seen God's son risen from the dead.'

When they looked up, Jesus was there, but he was alone with them. The two other men had gone.

279 THE STORY OF THE GOOD SAMARITAN

One day a man came to Jesus to see how he would answer questions about God's laws. He had heard that people followed Jesus because what he said about God was different from what the religious leaders taught.

'Teacher,' he said. 'What must I do to live with God for ever?'

'What does God's law say?' Jesus asked the man.

'Love God with all your heart, your soul, your strength and your mind. Love your neighbour as you love yourself,' replied the man.

'Do this and you will live with God for ever,' said Jesus.

'Who is my neighbour?' asked the man.

'I will tell you a story,' said Jesus. 'There was once a man who was walking on the lonely road from Jerusalem to Jericho. He was attacked by some robbers, who stole his money and took his clothes and left him half dead by the side of the road. Later, a priest came along the same road. He saw the injured man but decided not to help him. He walked past on the other side.

'Some time later, a Levite came along the road. He also saw the wounded man but did not stop to help.

'Finally, a Samaritan came along the road. As soon as he saw the man lying there, he stopped. He bandaged his wounds, helped him on to his own donkey and took him to an inn. He gave the innkeeper some money and asked him to look after the injured man until he was well again. "When I return I will give you any more money you need," he said.'

Then Jesus asked the man who was listening to the story:

'Who was a good neighbour to the wounded man?'

'The one who helped him,' said the man.

'You must do the same as him,' said Jesus.

280 MARY AND MARTHA

Jesus and his disciples passed through the little village of Bethany on their way to Jerusalem. A woman called Martha made them welcome and invited them in to eat with her.

Martha made herself busy in the kitchen, preparing the food and clearing up. She wanted everything to be just right for her visitors. Her sister Mary sat on the floor in the other room, listening to Jesus as he talked.

When Martha saw how Mary was doing nothing to help her, she felt cross.

'Lord,' she said to Jesus, 'Mary is just sitting there, doing nothing, while I am having to do all the work. Tell her to help me!'

Jesus looked at Martha.

'Martha,' he said, 'there is always something that has to be done. Sometimes it's good to stop and listen and spend time with people. Mary has chosen to do that now. Let her stay and listen.'

281 THE GOOD SHEPHERD

Many of the Pharisees and teachers of the law criticised Jesus because he spent time with ordinary people, many of whom they thought were sinners, doing things that were wrong.

'If you owned 100 sheep,' Jesus said to them, 'and one of them was lost, would you leave it to die? No, you would look everywhere until it was found, then you would be happier over that one lost sheep than over all the others. God cares about people the same way.'

'I am like a good shepherd,' Jesus also said. 'I know my sheep by name and care about them; they know my voice and that I will lead them to good pasture. I love my sheep and will let no harm come to them. When someone who is not a real shepherd looks after the sheep, he runs away if a wolf comes and attacks them. I am willing to die for my sheep.

'I am the good shepherd. I know my sheep and my sheep know me. I have other sheep too who are not in the same sheepfold. One day there will be one great flock, all led by one shepherd. I will lay down my life for the sheep; no one will take my life from me. Then I will take up my life again.'

'Whatever is he talking about?' some of the people said. 'Is Jesus mad?'

Others in the crowd tried to understand.

282 THE LOVING FATHER

Jesus told another story about God's love.

'There was once a man with two sons. One day, the younger son said to his father, "Let me have my share of everything I will inherit when you die. I'd like to travel and enjoy myself now." So the father divided everything that he had between his two sons.

'The younger son took his money and went far away. He used all his money enjoying himself and making lots of friends, but after a time he had spent it all.

'Then there was a terrible famine in the land. There was nothing to eat. The younger son took the only job he could find, feeding pigs. He was so hungry, he could have eaten the pigs' food. Then the young man realised how silly he was.

'"The people who work for my father have far more than I have now. I'll go home and tell him I am sorry. I will ask if I can have a job on the farm."

'The boy's father had been watching and waiting, hoping his son would come back. He saw his son coming and ran to meet him. He threw his arms around him and hugged him.

'"I have let you down and done things I am ashamed of,' the boy said. "I'm so sorry. I don't deserve to be treated as your son. Let me work for you instead."

His father shook his head.

'"Fetch the best clothes for my son," the father called to one of his servants. "Find new sandals and a ring for his finger. Prepare the best food. I thought my son was dead. He was lost, but now he's found. Let's have a party to celebrate his return!"'

283 THE MAN WHO HAD EVERYTHING

One day a man in the crowd listening to Jesus shouted out to him.

'Teacher, tell my brother to share his inheritance with me!'

'I am not here to settle family arguments,' Jesus replied. 'I am here to warn you about greed. Make sure you don't fall into the trap of thinking that your life is made up of the things you own. Life is worth so much more than that!

'Let me tell you a story. Once there was a rich farmer. His land produced an excellent harvest. He had so many crops he couldn't store them all. So he thought he would pull down his barns and build new, bigger barns. Then he could store everything he owned and rest and enjoy life. He could eat all he wanted, drink all he wanted and be happy.

'That night God said to him: "Tonight will be your last. It is your time to die. You have stored up many things on earth but now you must leave them all behind."

'What good was all the rich farmer's money to him after his death?' asked Jesus after the story was ended. 'None at all. This is what happens when people live their lives for themselves alone, thinking only of how many possessions they have. Live your lives for others, thinking of their needs before your own. God will look after you, and you will store treasure in heaven, where no moth can eat it and no thief steal it away.'

284 THE UNTOUCHABLES

As Jesus passed near the border of Samaria and Galilee, he saw ten men standing together in a huddle. They were dressed in rags and had covered their faces and their damaged limbs. Jesus knew that they had the skin disease called leprosy that made them outcasts.

They called to Jesus from a distance.

'Jesus! Please heal us!'

Jesus knew how much they suffered and wanted to help them.

'Go to the priest,' Jesus told them. 'Show him your skin.'

The ten men turned to walk away but as they did so, they realised that they had been healed. Their skin was healthy. The leprosy had gone!

One of the men was from Samaria. He turned back to Jesus, praising God, and knelt at Jesus' feet.

'Thank you, Master! Thank you!' he said.

Jesus looked at the man on his knees and he looked into the distance at those who were still walking away.

'Were there not ten men who needed help?' said Jesus. 'Are you the only one who came back to thank God? Go now. You are well because you believed that God could heal you.'

285 LIFE AFTER DEATH

Mary and Martha had a brother named Lazarus who was also one of Jesus' close friends. When Lazarus fell ill, the two sisters sent a message to Jesus, asking him for help.

Jesus was some distance away when he heard the message. By the time he got to Bethany, Lazarus was dead and had been buried for four days. There were many friends there, mourning his death and weeping with his sisters.

'If you had been here earlier, Lord, Lazarus would still be alive!' said Martha, going to meet him. 'Even now I know that God will give you whatever you ask for.'

'Lazarus will live again,' said Jesus. 'I am the resurrection and the life. If you believe in me, you will live for ever. Do you believe, Martha?'

'Yes, I do!' said Martha, and she ran to fetch her sister.

When Mary saw Jesus, she fell at his feet, weeping. Jesus knew how sad she was, and he cried with her. Then they took Jesus to the place where Lazarus was buried.

'Open the tomb!' he ordered.

'He's been dead for days!' cried Martha.

'Trust me, Martha,' said Jesus to her. Then Jesus prayed to God before calling to Lazarus.

Lazarus walked out of the tomb still wrapped up in his grave clothes.

'Take off his grave clothes and take him home,' said Jesus.

Mary and Martha were overjoyed to have their brother back. Many of their friends believed in Jesus because they had seen what had happened.

286 70 TIMES SEVEN

Peter had come to Jesus and asked him about forgiveness.

'How many times should I forgive someone if they wrong me?' he asked. 'Will seven times be enough?'

'No,' Jesus had replied. 'Not seven but 70 times seven. You must always be ready to forgive.'

Then Jesus told this story to explain.

'Imagine there is a king who wants to settle accounts with his servants. The first man came before him owing £10,000. He could not pay any of it. The king was ready to sell the man, his wife and his children into slavery and sell everything he owned so the debt could be paid, but the man begged him to let him have more time to pay. The king was more kind than the servant could have imagined. He cancelled the debt completely.

'The servant left the king, unable to believe how lucky he was, until he bumped into a man he knew who owed him £10. He grabbed the man by the neck and shouted at him.

'"Give me back what you owe me now!" he said.

'The man begged him to be patient. He needed more time to pay, but the servant would not listen. He had the man thrown into prison until he could pay back his debt.

'The other servants felt the servant had acted unfairly. They told the king, who called the man back.

'"I forgave you and cancelled your large debt because you begged me to. How could you not show the same kindness to the man who owed you a much smaller sum? Go to prison. Stay there until you can pay me back the very last penny."

'This,' said Jesus, 'is why you must forgive others from your heart whatever they have done. You need God's forgiveness too.'

287 THE PRAYERS GOD HEARS

Jesus once told this story to teach people how to pray.

'Two men went to the temple to pray to God. One was a Pharisee; the other a tax collector.

'"Thank you, God, for making me what I am," said the Pharisee in a loud voice. "I don't steal or break any of your laws. I am much better than this man here, one of the hated tax collectors! I give you a tenth of all I have and pray on an empty stomach twice a week to show you how good I am."

'The Pharisee was very pleased with himself. The tax collector bowed his head and mumbled his prayers in his shame. '"God, please forgive me and be kind to me, for I am a sinner, and I deserve nothing from you."

'God heard the prayers of both men,' said Jesus. 'But only the prayers of the tax collector were acceptable to him.'

288 JESUS BLESSES THE CHILDREN

The people who came to Jesus were not just those who were blind or deaf; not all of them were in need of his healing touch. Some came to Jesus just for his blessing.

When some parents brought their babies and small children to Jesus to be blessed, the disciples tried to send them away.

'Jesus is too busy,' they said. 'Take the children home.'

Jesus got down to the level of a small child and smiled.

'Come here,' he called to one. 'Let them all come.'

Then Jesus spoke to the disciples.

'God's kingdom belongs to people like this. Learn from them. They trust me and love me without question. No one can be part of God's kingdom without such simple trust.'

289 THE RICH YOUNG MAN

A young man who had great wealth came to Jesus and went on his knees.

'Good teacher, tell me please. How can I live for ever?'

'You must keep God's laws,' replied Jesus.

'I have done that since I was a boy,' said the man.

Jesus smiled kindly at the man. He saw what the problem was.

'There is one more thing you can do,' said Jesus. 'Sell everything you have, give your money to the poor, and follow me.'

The rich man suddenly looked sad. He got up and walked away. He was very wealthy. He could not do what Jesus asked. His money meant more to him than God.

Jesus looked at his friends.

'It is very hard for a rich man to enter God's kingdom. It is easier for a camel to go through the eye of a needle.'

290 THE GENEROUS MASTER

Jesus told the disciples a story about what God's kingdom was like.

'There was once a man who had many rows of vines, and plenty of work to be done. He went down to the marketplace early in the morning to hire some workers. He agreed to pay them a silver coin each as fair payment for the day.

'At nine o'clock in the morning the owner went to the marketplace and hired some more men. At midday the owner went a third time and hired yet more workers. He went again at three o'clock and then at five o'clock. Each time he hired more workers.

'When the day's work was ended, the men came to be paid. The owner told his foreman to start paying the men who were hired last first of all. Each of the men was paid a silver coin—the same amount whether he had been there a few hours or all day.

'"This is not fair!" grumbled one of the men who had started early in the morning. "I have worked in the hot sun all day but have no more for my trouble than those who came a short while ago." Others agreed. They were so unhappy that they complained to the owner.

'"What is your problem?" the owner asked. "I paid you what we agreed. I chose to give the same reward to everyone. Surely I have the right to share what I have in whatever way I choose?"

'This is the way God is,' said Jesus. 'He will not just be fair; he will be generous. Those who come last will still be rewarded.'

291 BLIND BARTIMAEUS

Bartimaeus was begging at the side of the road when Jesus and his friends went to Jericho. Bartimaeus was blind, but he heard the crowd who were following Jesus. He knew something unusual was happening.

'Who's passing by?' he shouted out. 'What's happening?'

'It's Jesus,' someone answered him. 'The teacher from Nazareth is here in Jericho!'

Bartimaeus had heard all about Jesus. He knew that he had made a paralysed man walk and helped a deaf man hear.

'Help me!' he shouted out. 'Jesus, have pity on me!'

'Be quiet!' said someone else in the crowd.

'Stop shouting!' said another.

Bartimaeus would not stop. He shouted even louder.

'Jesus! Help me!'

Jesus heard Bartimaeus and stopped.

'Tell him to come to me,' he said.

'It's OK!' someone told Bartimaeus. 'Jesus is asking for you!'

Bartimaeus threw off his cloak and jumped to his feet. He felt his way through the crowd until he came to Jesus.

'How can I help you?' asked Jesus.

'I want to see again,' said Bartimaeus.

'Then you shall see,' replied Jesus. 'Go now. You believed I could make you well. You can have what you asked for.'

Bartimaeus was blind no longer. He could see! He didn't return to his place on the roadside to beg. Now Bartimaeus joined the crowd of people following Jesus.

292 THE LITTLE TAX COLLECTOR

Further up the road, a crowd was gathering to hear Jesus speak. Zacchaeus, the tax collector, was among them.

Zacchaeus was not a very tall man, and because he cheated people when he collected their taxes, he was also unpopular. He wanted desperately to see Jesus but because he was short, he could see nothing over the heads of everyone else.

Then he had an idea. He went on ahead of the crowd and climbed a tree so that he could see Jesus coming down the road.

When Jesus reached the tree, he stopped.

'Zacchaeus!' said Jesus, looking up at him. 'Come down from the tree! I want to come to your house today.'

'You are welcome to stay with me, Jesus,' he said.

'Why stay with that cheat? Why even speak to him?' The people in the crowd were cross.

Zacchaeus wanted to put things right.

'Jesus!' he said in a loud voice. 'I'm going to give half of all I own to the poor. If I have cheated anyone, I will pay them back four times the amount.'

Jesus smiled at Zacchaeus.

'Today is a wonderful day!' he said. 'It is for this that I have come— to save people who had forgotten how to live God's way.'

293 THE END OF THE WORLD

Jesus talked to his disciples about how to love and serve God and other people. He also told them about a time in the future when God would send his angels to the whole earth to gather together all the people who loved him.

'No one knows when that time will come,' said Jesus, 'except God himself. People will be working right up to that time; they will be marrying and having children. When it happens, one person will be taken to be with God and another will be left behind. Make sure you are one of those who loves God. Be ready for that day to come.

'Let me tell you a story about ten bridesmaids,' said Jesus. 'Each one had a little oil lamp so she could welcome the bridegroom to the house that night. Five of the bridesmaids were prepared. They had brought some spare oil. The other five were not prepared.

'Hours passed and the bridegroom did not come. The bridesmaids grew tired with waiting and fell asleep.

'Then in the middle of the night, they heard a noise. "The bridegroom is coming! Wake up!" someone shouted.

'The bridesmaids picked up their lamps. The five who had brought the spare oil could light them; the lamps of the others had gone out and they had to go and get some more.

'While they were away, the bridegroom arrived. The other five bridesmaids held up their lamps and walked with him into the wedding feast. Then the door was shut.

'The other five were too late; they missed the wedding feast.'

294 THE FINAL JUDGMENT

Jesus told the disciples what would happen at the end of the world. He described it in this way:

'The king will sit on his throne surrounded by angels. He will divide all the people of the earth into two groups.

'"Come to me and enjoy all the good things I have prepared for you," the king will say to one group. "For you lived the way God wanted you to live. When I was hungry, you shared your food with me. When I was thirsty, you gave me a drink. You welcomed me into your home when you didn't know me and gave me clothes when I had none. You cared for me when I was ill and even came to visit me in prison."

'Then those people will say to the king, "When did we ever do these things? When did we see you hungry and feed you, thirsty and give you a drink? When did we clothe you, or welcome you into our homes, look after you in illness or visit you in prison?"

'Then the king will answer, "Whenever you helped someone in need, you did this for me."

'The king will turn to the other group and send them away. "You gave me no food when I was hungry; you let me die of thirst. You shut your door against me and wouldn't let me in. You saw that I needed clothes but you wouldn't help me and when I was ill and in prison, you had no time to take care of me."

'"When did we do these things?" the other group will say. "When did we ever see you in need – hungry or thirsty, in need of a home or clothes, ill or in prison?"

'The king will reply, "Whenever you saw someone in need and you walked by without helping them, you refused to help me."'

295 THE JAR OF PERFUME

A few days before the Passover, Lazarus invited Jesus to his home in Bethany.

Lazarus and the disciples sat with Jesus at the table while Martha served the food. Mary went to wash Jesus' feet, but instead of using water, as she would for any other guest, Mary poured out some expensive perfume. Then she wiped Jesus' feet with her long hair.

The room was filled with the beautiful smell of the perfume. Judas Iscariot watched and disapproved.

'What a waste!' he said. 'That perfume could have been sold and the money given to the poor.'

Judas wasn't being completely honest. He looked after the money that was given to support Jesus, but he often stole from the amount they collected to help others and spent it on himself. Jesus was sad at Judas' reaction.

'Leave Mary alone,' said Jesus. 'What she has done has prepared me for my burial. There will always be people in need of your help, but I will not be here with you for much longer.'

296 JESUS GOES TO JERUSALEM

Jesus and his friends went on to Jerusalem by way of Bethphage on the Mount of Olives. Jesus asked two of his disciples to go ahead and bring back a young donkey which would be waiting for them.

'If anyone asks what you are doing, tell them that I need it, and they will not stop you.'

The two friends did as Jesus asked. They found the young donkey and brought it to Jesus. They put a cloak on the back of the animal, which had never been ridden before. Then Jesus sat on its back and started to ride towards Jerusalem.

A large crowd gathered along the sides of the road. Some people spread their cloaks on the ground for the colt to walk on. Some cut huge palm branches from the trees and spread those over the road while others waved palm branches.

Everyone was shouting.

'Hosanna!' they cried. 'God bless the king!'

There were some Pharisees there watching and they spoke to Jesus.

'What nonsense is this?' they said to him. 'Stop these people. Make them be quiet!'

Jesus knew that this would be the last time he received such a welcome. The next crowd would be shouting something very different.

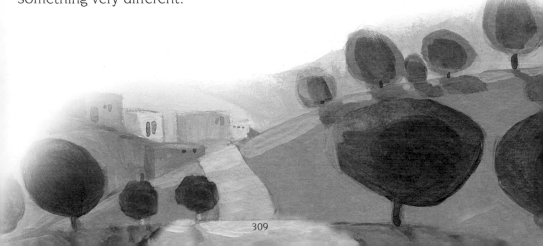

297 A DEN FOR THIEVES AND ROBBERS

Once inside the city, Jesus went into the temple courtyard. He saw the money changers and dove-sellers busy making money for themselves, and he was angry. Jesus took hold of one table after another, and overturned them. Money scattered everywhere.

'This is God's house!' he shouted. 'It is a place for people to pray and worship God, but you have made it into a dishonest marketplace, a den for thieves and robbers!'

Every day Jesus taught in the temple, surrounded by crowds of people not wanting to miss anything he said. Others came to him to be healed: the blind people, the deaf, those who couldn't walk or suffered from various illnesses. Anyone who needed Jesus came, and he healed them.

The chief priests and the Pharisees watched Jesus. They hated what he was saying and doing. They hated Jesus. Because of the love of the people, there was nothing they could do.

Little children danced around the temple courts singing:

'Hosanna! Praise Jesus! God has come to save us!'

298 THE GREATEST COMMANDMENT

The Pharisees and the Sadducees kept asking Jesus questions to see if they could find some fault with him.

'Tell me, which is the most important of all the commandments?' asked one of the teachers of the law.

'The most important of all is this,' said Jesus. 'The Lord our God is the only Lord. Love the Lord your God with all your heart, with all your soul, with all your mind and with all your strength. The second is this: Love your neighbour as yourself.'

'You are right,' said the teacher. 'To do these things is better than to offer sacrifices to God.'

Jesus looked at the man. He was pleased with the wisdom of his answer.

'If you understand this much, you are close to God's kingdom,' Jesus said to him. Then no one else dared to ask him anything else.

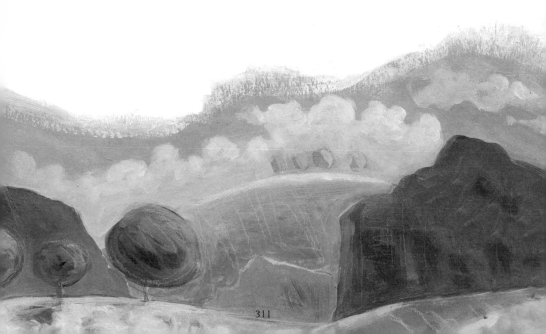

299 THE GREATEST GIFT

While he was in the temple, Jesus saw some rich men putting money into the temple treasury boxes. As he watched, a poor widow came and slipped two small copper coins into the box. Jesus turned to the people around him.

'That woman has given far more than anyone else,' he said. 'The men gave large gifts but these were a small proportion of what they had. They could well afford to give them; it didn't cost them much. That woman gave everything she had to God.'

300 THE PLOT TO KILL JESUS

The chief priests and the elders met together secretly.

'We can't let this go on any longer,' they said. 'We must find a way to destroy Jesus.'

'The people are on his side,' said one. 'Passover is only two days away and Jerusalem is too busy. If we have Jesus arrested now, there will be a riot!'

Meanwhile Judas Iscariot was also plotting. He went looking for some of the chief priests. 'What will you give me if I betray Jesus?' he asked.

'We will give you 30 silver coins,' they answered. This was the opportunity they needed—someone who could help them trap Jesus when he was alone.

Judas took their money. Now all he had to do was wait for the right moment.

301 THE UPSTAIRS ROOM

The people in Jerusalem were getting ready for the Passover feast. Jesus sent Peter and John to make arrangements for them.

'You'll meet a man carrying a water jar as you go into the city,' Jesus told them. 'Follow him. He will enter the house where we will celebrate the feast. Find the owner and ask him which room he has prepared for the Teacher and his disciples. He will show you a large furnished room upstairs. Then you can get everything ready.'

The two men went into the city and saw the man with the water jar. They went into the house with him and the owner took them to the upstairs room.

Everything was just as Jesus had told them. Then Peter and John started to get things ready for the special feast.

302 JESUS, THE SERVANT

The night before Passover, Jesus and his disciples met in the upstairs room to have supper. Jesus wrapped a towel around his waist and filled a basin with water and started to wash his friends' feet. It was usually the job of a servant. Peter refused to let Jesus do it.

'Peter, if I don't wash your feet, you cannot be my friend.'

'Then don't just wash my *feet*. Wash all of me!' said Peter.

'There's no need,' said Jesus. 'Only your feet are dirty.' His thoughts turned to Judas. 'Although that's not true of everyone here,' he added.

When Jesus had finished, he returned to the table with his disciples.

'Do you understand what I have just done?' Jesus asked them. 'I am your teacher, but I have just done the job of a servant. I want you to treat each other with that same love and respect. Follow my example.'

303 THE BETRAYER

Jesus ate with his friends but they could see that he was thoughtful and even unhappy. Then he spoke.

'One of you here is going to betray me,' he said.

The disciples looked at him in amazement. Then they looked at one another in disbelief.

'Ask him who it is,' mouthed Peter to John, who was next to Jesus.

John whispered to him, 'Who is it, Lord?'

'I will dip some bread in the sauce and give it to him,' Jesus told John. Then Jesus gave the bread to Judas.

'Go now,' Jesus said to him. 'Do what you have to do.'

Judas took the bread, stood up and made his way out of the room quietly into the darkness.

Then Jesus held the loaf of unleavened bread and thanked God for it. He broke it into pieces and shared it with his friends.

'Eat this. This is my body, which is given for you,' he said. 'Remember me whenever you eat bread together.' Then Jesus picked up a cup of red wine. 'Drink this. This wine is my blood, shed for you so that your sins may be forgiven.'

Jesus' friends ate and drank with him, but they did not understand what Jesus was telling them until after he had died.

304 SLEEPING FRIENDS

After supper, Jesus and his disciples walked to a nearby olive grove.

'All of you will run away and leave me tonight,' Jesus said. 'After I am raised from the dead, I will meet you in Galilee.'

'I will never leave you,' said Peter, 'even if all the others do.'

'Peter,' Jesus replied sadly, 'before the cock crows at first light, you will have denied three times that you even know me.'

'I would die first!' said Peter bravely and all the other disciples agreed with him.

Jesus told them to wait for him while he prayed. They saw that he was very sad.

'Father,' Jesus said, 'don't make me go through all the suffering ahead of me! But let me do what you want, not what I want.'

Then Jesus got up and walked back to his waiting friends, but he found they had all fallen asleep.

'Can't you even stay awake for one hour?' he asked. 'I know you want to help me, but you have no strength.'

Jesus went to pray again.

'Father, if I must suffer, then I am ready to obey you.'

When he went to his friends a second and third time, his friends had fallen asleep again. They could not keep their eyes open.

'Wake up!' said Jesus. 'It is time. Here is the man who has betrayed me.'

305 JESUS IS ARRESTED

The quiet of the dark olive grove gave way to the sound of people, a large crowd with clubs and swords in their hands. Leading them all was Judas Iscariot.

Judas walked straight up to Jesus and kissed him as if he were still his friend. It was the signal the crowd needed. They closed in around Jesus and held him so he could not move.

The disciples were afraid. One of them lashed out with a sword and cut off the ear of the high priest's servant.

'Put down that sword!' said Jesus, touching the man's ear and healing him. 'There's no need for violence. If I wanted help, I could ask God to send angels to rescue me. Why do you men need to use force to take me away? You could have come any day when I was teaching the people.'

They marched Jesus away to see Caiaphas, the high priest. Jesus' friends ran away, leaving him alone. Only Peter followed some distance away.

306 THE NEXT MORNING

There was a crowd seated around a fire in the courtyard of the high priest's house. Peter went in the darkness to sit with them.

Inside the house, the elders and teachers of the law had gathered to await Jesus' arrival. They talked among themselves, trying to find some reason to put him to death. They needed some crime to accuse him of but they could find none. Finally, the high priest asked Jesus if he were the Christ, the Son of God, whom everyone had been waiting for, the one the prophets had said God would send them.

'I am,' said Jesus, 'and I will soon be seated at God's right hand.'

'That's it! Blasphemy!' shouted Caiaphas. They had the reason they needed to ask the Romans for his execution.

Outside, a servant girl had been watching Peter in the firelight.

'I know you,' she said. 'You're one of Jesus' friends.'

'No, I'm not,' said Peter, getting to his feet. 'I don't even know him!'

Some time later a man noticed Peter there.

'I'm sure you were with Jesus,' he said.

'You're mistaken!' Peter replied angrily. 'I'm not his friend.'

Just before dawn, another man accused Peter.

'You come from Galilee too,' he said. 'I can tell by your accent. You must know Jesus.'

'I don't know what you're talking about!' Peter answered.

At that moment, a cock crowed. It was dawn, and Peter suddenly remembered what Jesus had said to him.

Peter rushed away and cried in shame at what he had done.

307 A MURDERER GOES FREE

Pontius Pilate, the Roman governor, stared thoughtfully at the man in front of him, bound and with his head bowed.

'You know that the chief priests want you dead,' Pilate said to Jesus. 'Have you nothing to say for yourself?'

Jesus stood silently. Pilate could find nothing under Roman law that would justify Jesus being punished by death, but he could see that the leaders of the people wanted some excuse for trouble. He decided to ask the crowd outside, who were waiting for his verdict.

'You know it is the custom at Passover to release a prisoner,' he said. 'Shall I release Barabbas, or Jesus, whom some believe is the Messiah, the chosen one?'

The chief priests and the elders had made sure their supporters were in the crowd.

'Barabbas!' they shouted. 'Set Barabbas free!'

'Then what shall I do with Jesus?' asked Pilate.

'Crucify him!' the men in the crowd shouted. 'Crucify him!'

Pilate looked down at their angry faces as they began to shout and wave their fists. He shook his head sadly and called for water to wash his hands in front of the crowd.

'This man's death is nothing to do with me,' he told them.

Pilate had Jesus taken away by soldiers to be crucified and he released Barabbas, the murderer.

308 THE KING OF THE JEWS

The Roman soldiers took away Jesus' clothes and dressed him in the scarlet cloak of a Roman soldier. They twisted together branches of sharp thorns into a crown and forced it down on his head so that blood trickled down his face. They put a stick in his right hand and knelt in front of him, laughing.

'Look! Here is the king of the Jews!' they sneered, spitting in his face. Then they took away the stick and beat him again and again.

When they were bored with making fun of Jesus, the soldiers gave him back his own clothes and took him away to be crucified.

Jesus was bruised and bleeding; he was exhausted from the beating. As he tried to carry the wooden bar on which he would be crucified, he stumbled and fell.

'You! Here!' they said to a man in the crowd. 'Carry this!'

The man, Simon from Cyrene, put the long piece of wood on his shoulder and followed Jesus to the place of execution outside the city walls.

309 THE PLACE OF THE SKULL

The route was lined with people. Some shouted and jeered; others watched sadly; yet more wept and cried to see Jesus taken away to Golgotha, the Place of the Skull.

Two other men were led out to be crucified that day, both of them thieves. Jesus was nailed to the wooden bar and hoisted up between them.

'Forgive them, Father!' said Jesus. 'They don't know what they are doing!'

The crowds watched and waited. The soldiers jeered.

'You saved other people, but you can't help yourself!' they said.

Some of the soldiers gambled for Jesus' clothes. One of the thieves who hung beside Jesus shouted to him.

'If you really are God's Son, then save us all!'

'Leave him!' said the other thief. 'We deserve our punishment but this man has done nothing wrong.' Then he spoke to Jesus. 'Remember me,' he said.

'Today you will be with me in paradise,' Jesus replied.

John, one of Jesus' disciples, was standing near the foot of the cross. Jesus' own mother was also there.

'Dear woman,' Jesus said to Mary, 'treat this man as your son. John,' he then said to his friend, 'treat this woman as if she were your mother.'

At midday the sky turned black. At around three o'clock in the afternoon, Jesus called out loud:

'It is finished!' and breathed his last breath.

310 SECRET FOLLOWERS

Joseph of Arimathea was a member of the Jewish Council, the Sanhedrin. Like Nicodemus, he was a secret follower of Jesus, and neither man had been among those who plotted to kill him.

As it was almost the sabbath, Joseph went to Pontius Pilate and asked if Jesus' body could be taken down from the cross and buried.

Pilate was surprised that Jesus was already dead and checked first with the guards. Then, with Pilate's permission, Joseph went with Nicodemus and took Jesus' broken body from the cross. There were wounds in his hands and feet, and in his side where a soldier had stabbed him with a sword to check that he was dead.

The men wrapped Jesus in strips of linen with myrrh and aloes, and placed his body in the newly made tomb that Joseph had prepared for his own burial. Then they rolled a great stone across the entrance to seal it.

Mary Magdalene and her friend sat nearby and watched where they put Jesus' body.

311 THE EMPTY TOMB

Mary Magdalene wanted to anoint Jesus' body with spices. She hadn't been able to do it on Friday or Saturday because it was not allowed on the sabbath day. So she went at sunrise on Sunday.

When she arrived in the garden, she saw that the huge stone that had been in front of the tomb had been rolled away. The tomb was empty. Mary ran back to find Peter and John.

'They've taken Jesus away!' she cried.

Peter and John ran to the tomb to see if there could be any mistake. They saw the linen cloths but Jesus was not there. The two men ran home, leaving Mary alone in the garden.

Mary was still weeping when she went to look inside the tomb again. This time she saw two angels.

'Why are you crying?' asked one of the angels.

'They have taken my master away,' Mary sobbed. 'I don't know where they have put him!'

Mary turned as she heard someone else behind her.

'Who are you looking for?' the man asked.

'Please, just tell me where his body is,' she said.

The man answered with just one word.

'Mary,' he said. Mary knew straight away who the man was. It was Jesus!

'Master!' she said, overjoyed to see him.

'Go and tell the others what you have seen,' he said.

Mary ran all the way.

'I have seen Jesus!' she said. 'He's no longer dead. He's alive!'

312 THE ROAD TO EMMAUS

Later that same day, two of Jesus' followers were walking along the road from Jerusalem to the village of Emmaus. They were talking together about all the events of the last few days.

As they walked, another man came alongside them. 'What are you talking about?' he asked them.

Cleopas looked at the stranger, surprised.

'Surely you must have heard what has happened?' he said. 'We were talking about Jesus of Nazareth. We thought he was the Saviour God had promised to us. Three days ago, our chief priests and elders had him executed. Then today we have heard that his tomb is empty. They say he has risen from the dead!'

The stranger then began to explain all that the prophets had told the people about God's Saviour, about how he had to suffer and die.

It was almost dark when they reached Emmaus.

'Come,' said Cleopas to the stranger. 'Stay here with us and have something to eat.'

As they sat down to share a meal together, the stranger picked up the bread, thanked God for it and broke it. Suddenly the two friends knew who the stranger was. They had been walking and talking with Jesus! They left everything and rushed back to Jerusalem to tell the others that Jesus was alive.

313 BEHIND LOCKED DOORS

When they arrived with their news, they found that the other disciples were together behind locked doors, talking about Jesus.

'Jesus is alive!' they said. 'He appeared today and spoke to Peter.'

'We've seen him too,' Cleopas told them. 'He walked with us to Emmaus and told us how he had to suffer and die before he could be raised. We didn't recognise him until he broke the bread!'

At that moment, Jesus stood with them in the room.

'Peace be with you,' he said.

At first they were afraid, but Jesus held out his hands and showed them the wounds where the nails had been.

'It really is you!' cried his disciples. 'You're alive!'

Then, because he said he was hungry, they gave him some cooked fish, which he ate in front of them.

Jesus reminded the disciples what they must do next.

'Start in Jerusalem,' he said. 'Tell people that I died and rose again. Tell them they must repent of their sins and that now they can be forgiven. Then go out to all nations and tell them too!'

314 THOMAS DOUBTS HIS FRIENDS

Thomas had not been there when Jesus appeared to his disciples in the upper room.

'I don't believe it!' said Thomas. 'I won't believe that Jesus is alive, unless I see him for myself and touch his wounds.'

A week later, Thomas and the others met together. As before, the doors were locked to protect them from Jesus' enemies. And, as before, Jesus appeared as if from nowhere and stood among them.

'Peace be with you,' he said. Then he turned to Thomas. 'Look at my hands, Thomas. Touch them. Look at the place where the sword cut my side. Touch that too. Now stop doubting and believe!'

Thomas sank to his knees. He knew that this was no ghost. Jesus was real and he was alive.

'My Lord and my God,' he said.

315 FISHING ON LAKE GALILEE

For a few weeks after Jesus' death, the disciples did not know what to do. One evening Peter was back at Lake Galilee and he decided to go fishing with some of his friends. He still could not forget that he had let Jesus down so badly and denied even knowing him.

They fished all night but caught nothing. As dawn came, they sailed back to the shore.

A man was standing on the beach watching them.

'Have you caught anything?' he called out.

'No,' they replied.

'Try throwing your nets on the right side of the boat.'

The fishermen did as the man suggested. Immediately, they felt the tug of the net as it filled with fish.

Peter looked at the man on the beach.

'It's Jesus!' he shouted. He jumped into the water and waded ashore.

Jesus had made a small fire and had some bread there. 'Bring some of the fish you have caught,' he said.

So the disciples dragged the net on to the shore and sat down with Jesus on the beach.

'Come,' said Jesus. 'Let's have breakfast together.'

316 PETER'S TASK

When breakfast was over, Jesus took Peter to one side to talk to him alone.

'Simon Peter,' he said, 'do you really love me?'

'You know I do,' said Peter.

'Then take care of my lambs,' Jesus replied.

A few minutes later, Jesus spoke again.

'Peter,' he said, 'do you truly love me?'

'Yes,' said Peter. 'You know I do!'

'Then take care of my sheep,' said Jesus.

After a little while, Jesus spoke for a third time.

'Peter,' he said, 'do you love me?'

Peter was hurt. He remembered how he had disowned Jesus, how he had let him down. He loved Jesus so much.

'You know everything,' he said to Jesus. 'You know that I love you.'

'I have a special job for you to do,' said Jesus. 'When I have gone away, I want you to look after my followers.'

317 JESUS RETURNS TO HEAVEN

After Jesus rose from the dead, his disciples saw him many times and in different places. Jesus taught them more about God. They had no doubt that he was the same Jesus they had known before his crucifixion. They knew that he was alive.

'Stay in Jerusalem,' he told them. 'Wait there, because I will send the Holy Spirit to you. Then go and tell people everywhere about me. Teach them everything I have done and said. I promise that I will always be there to help you.'

The apostles had often heard Jesus talk about the Holy Spirit, and how he would come to be with them after Jesus had gone.

About six weeks after Jesus rose from the dead, the apostles were with him on the Mount of Olives.

'When the Holy Spirit comes, you will have power,' Jesus said. 'The whole world will hear about me, because you will tell them. You will be my messengers.'

Then Jesus was covered by a cloud and seemed to rise up and disappear while they stood and stared.

Jesus had gone.

'What are you looking for?' asked two angels, standing among them. 'Jesus has gone back to heaven, but one day he will return.'

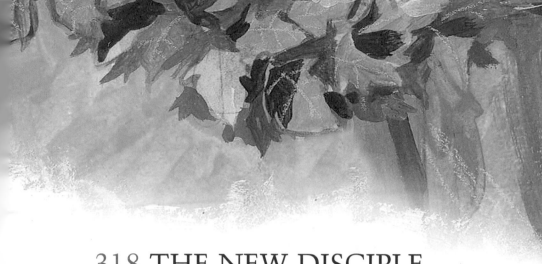

318 THE NEW DISCIPLE

The eleven friends returned to Jerusalem. They usually met to pray with some of the other believers. Now they called everyone together. There were about 120 people there.

'My friends,' Peter said to them. 'We have lost a member of our group. Judas was with us from the beginning; he was chosen to learn with us and work with us. He led the authorities to Jesus and betrayed him. Now he is dead.'

All the people there knew that Judas Iscariot had realised that he had done a terrible thing by betraying Jesus. Judas had taken his own life and had died in the field that the chief priests had bought with his 30 pieces of silver.

'We must find someone to replace Judas. The person must be one who has seen all we have seen and been with us from the start.'

Two men were suggested from the group. Then they all prayed, asking God to help them to choose the right person. Matthias then became the twelfth man, now known as apostles rather than disciples. They were not just those who followed and learned from their master; they had been sent out with his authority to speak and act in the name of Jesus.

319 THE POWER OF THE HOLY SPIRIT

Jerusalem was full of visitors from all over the world. They had come for the festival of Pentecost.

The disciples and other believers were together in one room when, suddenly, a sound like a strong wind blew through the house, filling it with noise. Something like flames seemed to burn in the air and touch each person there. As the Holy Spirit touched them, they all began to speak in other languages.

'What's happening?' People outside could hear the noise coming from the room. 'These people are speaking in my language, talking about God. How is this possible?'

Then Peter came to speak to the crowd. He told them that Jesus, the man who had been beaten and crucified, had risen from the dead, and that he was the Messiah, God's chosen one.

'What shall we do?' the people asked.

'Turn from your sins and be baptised,' Peter told them. 'You will be forgiven and will receive the Holy Spirit as we have.'

That day 3000 people became followers of Jesus. The apostles performed many miracles in the name of Jesus, and they met together with the other believers to worship God, to pray and to share what they had with each other.

320 THE MAN BY THE BEAUTIFUL GATE

One afternoon, as Peter and John went to the temple to pray, they passed a man begging at the Beautiful Gate. He held out his hands.

'Have you anything to spare?' he asked them hopefully.

Peter stopped and looked at him. The man had not been able to walk in more than 40 years. He was carried there to where he sat, day after day, hoping to be given enough money so that he could feed himself.

'I have no silver or gold,' said Peter, taking the man by his hands, 'but I can give you something much more. In the name of Jesus, stand up and walk!'

The man stood up with Peter's help. Once on his feet, he took some steps and then jumped in the air with joy.

'Praise God!' he shouted. 'I am healed. I can walk!'

Peter and John carried on towards the temple, smiling, but the man would not let them go.

The people all around stared, amazed.

'Isn't that the beggar who sat by the gate?' they asked each other. 'How is it that he can walk?'

333

321 PETER AND JOHN IN PRISON

Peter gave the people the answer they needed: it was faith in Jesus that had enabled them to help the beggar. The same Jesus whom they had crucified had risen from death and was waiting in heaven until the time when there would be a new heaven and earth.

The people listened to all he had to say until the temple guards and Sadducees came to see what was happening. Once they heard that Peter was telling everyone that Jesus had risen from the dead, they put both Peter and John in prison. The Sadducees taught that there was no resurrection of the dead.

Many believed what Peter had said and joined the growing number of people who called themselves Christians.

'How did you do this?' the high priest demanded of them next day. 'How was the man healed?'

'He was healed in the name of Jesus,' Peter said. 'Jesus is the man you crucified and God brought back to life.'

The high priest and elders could not understand how the man had been healed or how Peter, an uneducated fisherman, could speak to them with such authority.

They had to let Peter and John go, but they warned them not to talk about Jesus any more.

'We can do nothing else!' Peter and John replied. 'Which would you do? Obey God or obey people?'

When Peter and John returned to their friends, they asked for God's help to speak about Jesus, whatever happened to them.

322 GAMALIEL'S ADVICE

Wherever the apostles went, people brought out their friends or family to meet them. The streets were lined with those who were ill. The people in the nearby villages heard what was happening and people in need of help were brought to them.

The high priest and the Sadducees saw how many were being healed and how the number of believers was growing. They were very angry and locked up the apostles in the public jail.

During the night an angel opened the gates and led them out.

'Go to the temple,' the angel said. 'Tell everyone about the new life God has given you.'

Next morning the high priest and elders met to decide what to do with the prisoners when the news came of their disappearance.

'The prison doors are still locked, the guards are on duty but the men we arrested are no longer in the prison.'

'I have seen your prisoners,' said a man who had come from the temple. 'They are in the temple, teaching the people.'

Men were sent to bring them back without causing a riot.

'We told you not to talk about Jesus!' the high priest shouted. 'You not only disobeyed us, you are blaming us for his death!'

'We obeyed God,' replied Peter. 'Our sins have been forgiven; we must share this news with everyone.'

The Sanhedrin wanted the apostles executed.

'Leave them alone,' Gamaliel said. 'if this comes from God, if it is what they say it is, nothing we can do will stop it.'

The Sanhedrin listened to Gamaliel. They had the apostles beaten and set free. As soon as the apostles left, they continued to teach the people about Jesus.

323 STEPHEN IS KILLED

Now that there were so many believers, the apostles needed help to share out all they had so that no one was in need. Seven wise men were chosen, Stephen among them.

Stephen had been blessed by God with a number of special gifts and had healed many of the people. One day, some of Stephen's enemies, jealous of his wisdom and power, accused him of blasphemy in an attempt to get rid of him.

Stephen knew that blasphemy was a serious crime, but he listened calmly to the lies spoken against him before the Sanhedrin. His face shone like the face of an angel.

When it was his turn to speak in his defence, Stephen told them all about God's plan to save his people, from the time of Abraham. His closing words made them cover their ears in their anger.

'You are as stubborn as our ancestors! God has tried to speak to you but you have rejected him. God has sent Jesus to you but you had him killed. Now you reject the gift of the Holy Spirit!'

They marched Stephen outside the city and cast down their cloaks at the feet of a man called Saul. Then they pelted Stephen with stones until he fell to his knees.

'Lord Jesus,' said Stephen, 'forgive them for this sin and receive my spirit!' Then Stephen died.

Saul watched Stephen's death with interest. He was pleased that Stephen was no longer a threat.

324 SAUL, THE ENEMY

Stephen's friends went to collect his body and buried him, and there was great sorrow and sadness at his death.

There was little enough time to think about it. That very day, Saul and the authorities set about destroying the Christian believers. Saul went from house to house, dragging out from their homes any who believed, men and women, and locking them up in prison.

The Christians were scattered. Some hid from their persecutors; others moved away from Jerusalem. Wherever they went, they told people about the good news of Jesus.

Philip, another of the seven men who had been chosen to help the apostles, went to Samaria. He shared all he knew of Jesus with the people there and many came to hear him speak. People who were ill or paralysed came and were healed by him and many more were baptised in Jesus' name.

325 AN ANGEL SENDS PHILIP

Philip was still in Samaria when an angel spoke to him.

'Get ready to travel south to Gaza,' the angel told him.

Philip was passed by a man seated in a carriage, the treasurer of Queen Candace of Ethiopia. He had been to Jerusalem to worship God and was now reading the words of the prophet Isaiah.

The Holy Spirit prompted Philip to go over to the man's carriage and walk along beside it. The Ethiopian was looking puzzled.

'I need someone to explain these words to me,' the man said. Then he invited Philip into the carriage to travel with him.

'"Like a sheep that goes to be slaughtered, like a lamb that goes to have its wool cut off, he was silent and did not complain,"' he read aloud. '"He was treated unjustly, his life was ended before its time." Who is the prophet speaking of?' the man asked.

So Philip explained that Isaiah knew about the Saviour who would be taken and killed and would die in the place of all sinners.

'He is talking about Jesus, who died so that all who believe can be forgiven,' said Philip.

The Ethiopian treasurer now understood and believed.

'Here is a river,' the Ethiopian said. 'Will you baptise me?'

Both men went into the water and Philip baptised him. The man continued his journey happy, but he never saw Philip again.

326 SAUL, THE CHANGED MAN

Saul continued to look for all Christian believers, to stop them preaching about Jesus. He hated them and wanted to destroy them all.

'I want to go to Damascus,' Saul told the high priest. 'I need letters of introduction to the synagogues so I can find and arrest any Christians I find there.'

Saul set out along the road with some companions. When the city was finally in sight, a bright light from the sky suddenly dazzled him. Saul fell to the ground and heard a voice coming from nowhere.

'Saul, Saul, why are you persecuting me?'

'Who are you?' asked Saul.

'I am Jesus, the one you are persecuting,' said the voice. 'Get up and go to Damascus, and you will be told what to do next.'

Saul got to his feet but found that he could not see. His companions were as confused as he was. They had also heard the voice but seen no one. They led him by the hand into the city of Damascus. Saul's sight did not return for three days. He ate nothing during that time but spent his time praying.

327 A NEW LIFE

Meanwhile, Jesus spoke to a Christian believer in Damascus called Ananias.

'Ananias, I want you to go to Straight Street and call on Judas. There is a man there from Tarsus called Saul. He is blind and is praying. He has seen in a vision you touching him and restoring his sight.'

'Lord, I know of this man! He hates all Christians and has come here to destroy us,' Ananias replied.

'I know all this and I have chosen him to suffer for my sake,' said Jesus. 'He will tell my people and the Gentiles and even kings about me.'

So Ananias went to find Saul and placed his hands on him.

'Brother,' said Ananias, 'Jesus himself has sent me here so that you will see again and be filled with the Holy Spirit.'

Saul was able to see again! He was baptised and given something to eat. Then he stayed with the believers for a few days.

328 ESCAPE BY NIGHT

Saul went to the synagogue and preached.

'Jesus is the Son of God,' he said. 'Jesus is the Messiah!'

The people who heard him were amazed.

'Isn't this the man who killed Christians in Jerusalem?' they asked. 'We thought he had come here to do the same, yet now he speaks like one of them!'

Soon the Jews were plotting to kill Saul. They put guards on the city gates so he could not escape, but Saul had friends. One night they lowered him in a basket down through a gap in the city walls.

Saul went back to Jerusalem and tried to find the believers so he could join them, but they were afraid of Saul. Barnabas went with him to the apostles and explained what had happened to Saul on the road to Damascus.

'I have seen Jesus for myself,' Saul told them.

Saul went into Jerusalem and preached to the Greek-speaking Jews there until they too wanted to kill him.

Then the apostles helped him escape to Caesarea and sent him back to Tarsus, his home town.

329 AENEAS AND TABITHA

Meanwhile Peter travelled to many places, teaching and encouraging any Christian believers he found.

Once he went to Lydda where he met a man called Aeneas who had been paralysed for eight years.

'You are healed in the name of Jesus Christ,' Peter said to him.

Aeneas was able to get up and walk from that moment. Many people in Lydda put their trust in God.

The news of what Peter had done reached Joppa near the coast. The Christians in Joppa were very sad because their friend, Tabitha, had just died. Tabitha had been kind to everyone who was poor or in need. So the believers asked Peter to come and visit them.

Peter walked the twelve miles to Joppa and went to the place where Tabitha's body lay. All the friends were there, weeping and talking at once and making him look at all the beautiful clothes that Tabitha had made while she was alive. Peter sent everyone out of the room, then prayed for a while in the silence. Then he turned to the body and spoke.

'Tabitha, get up!'

She opened her eyes and sat up when she saw Peter there. Peter let the women come back into the room. He saw how happy they all were that Tabitha was alive again.

Everyone soon heard what had happened and many more people became Christians because of it. Peter then stayed in Joppa for a while at the house of a tanner called Simon.

330 AN ANGEL IN CAESAREA

The headquarters of the Roman forces occupying Judea were about 30 miles north of Joppa in the city of Caesarea. Cornelius was a Roman centurion in the Italian regiment stationed there.

Cornelius loved God and prayed to him regularly. He was also kind and generous to the poor, but he did not know about Jesus.

One afternoon, Cornelius was praying at the normal time of three o'clock in the afternoon when he saw an angel who called to him by name.

'What do you want from me?' Cornelius asked the angel.

'God has heard your prayers and seen how well you have treated those in need around you,' the angel replied. 'God wants you to invite a man called Peter here. You will need to send someone to Simon's home to find him. Simon is a tanner and his house is by the sea in Joppa.'

When the angel had gone, Cornelius called two of his servants and one of his soldiers who also believed in God. He told them what he had seen and then sent them to Joppa to find Peter.

331 THE ROOFTOP VISION

While the men were travelling to Joppa, Peter was praying on the rooftop of Simon's house. Then Peter saw a vision of a large sheet being lowered down by its four corners in front of him. The sheet was full of creatures that were good to eat, but also those that were forbidden according to Jewish law.

'Here is food for you, Peter. Prepare it and eat,' said God.

'I can't!' said Peter. 'Some of these animals are unclean and forbidden.'

'You don't need to call them unclean any longer. I have made them clean,' said God. The sheet came and went three times in Peter's vision.

Peter did not have long to sit and think about what the vision might mean.

'Three men are at the gate looking for you,' the Holy Spirit said to him. 'I have sent them. Don't be afraid to go with them.'

Peter went downstairs and met the three men who had just arrived and were asking for him.

'I am Peter,' he greeted them. 'Why are you here?'

When the men explained about the angel who had spoken to Cornelius, Peter invited them in to stay until the next morning. He was beginning to understand the meaning of his vision.

332 GOD'S BLESSING FOR ALL PEOPLE

Peter travelled to Caesarea the next day with some of the other believers. When they arrived at Cornelius' house, they found that he had invited all his family and friends to hear what Peter had to say.

'You know that Jewish law forbids a Jew to come into a Gentile's house. I am here because God has shown me that he does not have favourites; God accepts anyone who comes to him and wants to do what is right, no matter where they are from, no matter what their background is.' Then Peter told them everything he knew about Jesus.

While Peter was speaking, the Holy Spirit blessed all the people there. Cornelius and all the people believed that Jesus had died and risen so that their sins could be forgiven; they praised God and spoke in unknown languages. So Peter arranged for all of them to be baptised.

The believers who were with Peter were amazed. They all saw that what Peter had said was true: God's invitation was to everyone, whoever they are.

333 DEATH AND IMPRISONMENT

King Herod started to persecute the believers. First he arrested them; then he executed James, John's brother, who had been one of Jesus' first followers; then he put Peter in prison.

The night before Peter's trial, there were soldiers outside the prison cell and there were soldiers on either side of Peter as he sat in chains. All his friends in Jerusalem prayed for Peter.

Then, while Peter was asleep, his prison cell was filled with bright light as an angel woke him. The chains fell from his wrists and the prison gates opened as the angel led Peter past the guards.

Once in the street, the angel disappeared and Peter, who had thought it was all a dream, went to the house where everyone was praying. Peter knocked at the door and Rhoda, the servant girl, recognised his voice. She ran to the others and told them he was outside. At first no one believed her but Peter kept on knocking. When they opened the door and found that he was there, they could hardly believe it! God had answered their prayers.

Peter told them to explain what had happened to the other believers and then he went away so that Herod would not find him. Herod was furious when he found that Peter was gone, and he had the guards executed. No one could tell him how it happened.

334 THE MISSION TO CYPRUS

There were many Christians in Antioch in Syria. After Stephen's death, some of the believers had gone there to escape persecution and they had told people there about Jesus.

Barnabas was sent there to encourage them and he brought Saul to join him from Tarsus.

Then one day the believers heard the Holy Spirit telling them that Saul and Barnabas had been chosen to take the message about Jesus to the people on the island of Cyprus in the Mediterranean Sea. John Mark went with them.

They travelled over the island, teaching in the synagogues. When they reached Paphos, they met a sorcerer called Elymas, who worked for the Roman governor, Sergius Paulus. The governor sent for Saul and Barnabas because he wanted to hear about God, but Elymas did not want them to talk to his master.

'You mustn't listen to them!' he told the governor.

Saul, who was now known as Paul, looked straight at Elymas.

'You are full of tricks and deceit,' Paul said. 'You are an enemy of God and all his work. To stop you interfering in God's work you will now lose your sight.'

From that moment Elymas went blind. He could do nothing without someone to lead him. Sergius Paulus saw what had happened and was amazed. He believed in the power of Jesus.

335 A BRUTAL ATTACK

John Mark went back to Jerusalem while Paul and Barnabas sailed to Galatia.

In Lystra, a man sat listening to Paul as he talked about Jesus. The man had never been able to walk but began to believe that Jesus could heal him. Paul saw that the man had faith.

'Stand up and walk!' said Paul, looking straight at him.

There was an uproar as the crowd watched the man get up and walk among them.

'Here are Zeus and Hermes! The gods are here among us!' the crowd cried out. Then one of the Greek priests came with garlands and tried to prepare sacrifices for Paul and Barnabas.

'Stop this!' Paul shouted. 'We are here to tell you not to worship worthless things but the God who made heaven and earth. We are God's messengers, human, as you are.'

Still the crowd would not listen until some Jews came among them. They persuaded the crowd that Paul and Barnabas had come to deceive them. The mood of the crowd changed. Soon they were stoning Paul in an angry attack until he collapsed. Paul lay motionless on the ground until the men dragged his body outside the city.

Paul's friends came to his aid. He returned to the city but left Lystra with Barnabas the next day.

336 THE COUNCIL IN JERUSALEM

With so many people coming to believe in Jesus, disagreements began to arise about how best to follow him. Paul and Barnabas argued with some in Antioch who said that the Gentile Christians had to be circumcised as Moses had taught. Paul and Barnabas were sent to Jerusalem to discuss the matter with the leaders there.

'The Holy Spirit knows what goes on inside everyone,' Paul said. 'He came to Gentiles and blessed them just as he came to the Jewish believers. We are all saved because of God's grace alone.'

Eventually the leaders there agreed what should be taught to everyone. They gave a letter to Paul and Barnabas to take to the believers in Antioch.

'Paul and Barnabas come with our love and good advice,' the letter said. 'We are agreed that there is no need for circumcision when Gentiles become Christians but they should avoid food sacrificed to idols.'

Paul and Barnabas took the letter and stayed for a while in Antioch, teaching the people there.

When the time came to move on, Barnabas wanted to take John Mark with them but Paul did not. The two men agreed to work in different places. Barnabas went with John Mark to Cyprus, while Paul went with Silas to Syria and Cilicia.

337 FREE TO LOVE

Paul wrote to the Christians in Galatia about how they should worship God:

'You are children of God because of your faith. There is no difference between the Jewish believer and the Gentile believer; between the believer who is a slave and the believer who is a free man; between the male believer and the female believer. Once you are a Christian, you are all the same. You are all equally descendants of Abraham and will receive all the blessings that God promised him. God has given you the Holy Spirit as proof of that—the Spirit that cries out to God and knows that he is your loving Father.

'So you are all free—free to love and serve God as equals. This freedom is not so that you can behave badly but so that you can love each other as Jesus showed us how to love others. Don't become a slave to your human nature but let your lives be controlled by the Holy Spirit, producing love, joy, peace, patience, kindness, goodness, faithfulness, humility and self-control.'

338 PAUL BAPTISES LYDIA

Paul and Silas met Timothy, the son of a Jewish Christian mother and a Greek father, among the Christians in Lystra. Paul invited Timothy to join them.

Everywhere they went they encouraged those who already believed. They told others about Jesus, so that more and more people became followers. Soon they were also joined by a doctor named Luke.

During this time Paul had a vision in which he saw a man from Macedonia asking for help. The friends decided to go there on the next stage of their journey.

They stayed in Philippi for several days. On the sabbath they went outside the city to the river where the Jews met to pray. Paul sat down and began to speak about Jesus to some women who had gathered there.

Lydia was a businesswoman, a trader in expensive purple cloth. She already worshipped God, but as she listened to Paul and heard what he said about Jesus, she understood and believed that Jesus was God's Son.

After she and her family had been baptised, she invited Paul and his friends to stay as guests in her home.

339 THE FORTUNE-TELLER

There was a slave girl in Philippi who earned money for her owners by telling fortunes.

Wherever Paul and his friends went, the girl followed them.

'These men are servants of the Most High God,' she told anyone who would listen. 'They can tell you how to be saved.'

Paul knew that the girl had an evil spirit in her and he wanted to help her.

'In the name of Jesus, come out of her!' he ordered.

The girl was healed immediately; all her supernatural powers left her. When her owners realised what had happened, they were very angry. Now she was worth nothing to them!

The girl's owners took Paul and Silas to the marketplace and reported Paul and Silas as troublemakers. The crowd supported the girl's owners and the magistrates ordered that Paul and Silas be beaten and thrown in prison, to be guarded carefully.

The jailer made sure Paul and Silas had their feet fastened in the stocks in an inner cell. There would be no escape for them.

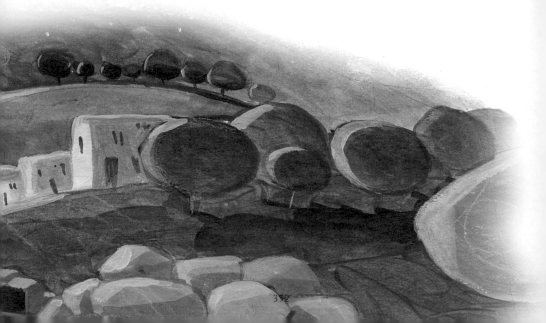

340 THE VIOLENT EARTHQUAKE

It was night. The prisoners were in darkness. Paul and Silas prayed and sang songs to God. Suddenly, every door in the prison burst open and the prisoners' chains came loose. A violent earthquake had shaken the foundations of the prison.

The jailer had been sleeping. When the earthquake woke him, he thought his prisoners had escaped. He drew his sword to kill himself in a panic.

'It's all right! We're all here,' shouted Paul.

The jailer stopped and brought lights so he could see.

'Tell me how I can be saved,' he asked.

'Trust Jesus,' said Paul, 'and you and your family will be saved.'

The jailer treated the wounds the men had received from their beatings and asked to be baptised. Then he took Paul and Silas to his home and prepared a meal for them.

In the morning the jailer received a message that the men could be released, but Paul was angry. He told the officers who had come that they were Roman citizens and could not be treated so unjustly.

The magistrates had not realised they were Roman citizens, and were frightened. They led them out of the prison, hoping there would be no more trouble. Then Paul and Silas went to Lydia's house for a while where they met with their friends before leaving Philippi.

341 THE UNKNOWN GOD

When Paul talked about Jesus in Thessalonica, he caused a riot among some of the Jews. His friends encouraged him to go on alone until they could join him.

While he waited for them, Paul walked the streets of Athens, amazed to see how many idols the Greeks there worshipped. In the synagogue Paul talked to the Jews; and in the marketplace he talked to the Gentiles; soon he was taken to the council of the Areopagus.

'Tell us about your ideas,' they invited him. 'These are new to us. We have never heard anything like them.'

'People of Athens,' he started, 'I can see that you are a very religious people. As I walked around your city I saw many objects of your worship. I even saw an altar to an unknown god. Now you worship him as unknown, but I know all about this God.

'The living God who made the earth and everything in it is so great he does not need to live in a temple made by the people he created. God himself gives us life and provides everything that we need. God made us so that we would seek him and find him, and he gave us his Son, Jesus, who rose from the dead, so that our sins could be forgiven.'

The people listened. Some wanted him to come back and tell them more; some sneered at his message and thought it nonsense; but some, Dionysius and Damaris among them, believed him and became followers of Jesus.

342 TENTMAKERS IN CORINTH

Paul went from Athens to Corinth where he met a tentmaker named Aquila and his wife Priscilla. They were among the Jews who had been ordered by Emperor Claudius to leave Rome. Paul stayed and worked with them, cutting and sewing goats' hair cloth to make tents.

Week by week, Paul went to the synagogue to preach and explain that Jesus was the one they had been waiting for, but few would listen and most were angry with Paul. So Paul spent most of his time in Corinth with Gentiles, who became believers and were baptised.

When Paul left Corinth for Ephesus, he took Priscilla and Aquila with him. He left them there while he sailed to Antioch.

Priscilla and Aquila then welcomed Apollos, an Alexandrian Jew, into their home. Apollos was a believer and preached in the synagogue but Priscilla and Aquila were able to encourage him and teach him more because of the time they had spent with Paul.

343 PAUL GOES TO EPHESUS

When Paul returned to Ephesus, he met twelve believers who had never heard of the Holy Spirit, even though they had been baptised. Paul explained to them about Jesus and when he put his hands on them, they were filled with the Holy Spirit.

For the next two years, Paul preached in the synagogue, read the scriptures and talked in public places. God worked through Paul so that many sick people were cured and believers also saw the power of God making them more like Jesus.

Then one day Demetrius, the silversmith, called together all the other craftsmen who made items to help people worship Artemis.

'This man Paul could stop us earning money,' Demetrius said. 'He tells people that there are no man-made gods, and lots of people, in Ephesus and beyond, believe him. We could lose our jobs and the great goddess Artemis will be forgotten.'

'Artemis is great!' the craftsmen chanted. Soon there was a riot and the crowd seized two of Paul's friends and dragged them to the theatre. Eventually an official stopped the riot.

'Ephesians!' he shouted. 'Our city is well known as the home of the great goddess Artemis. These men have done nothing wrong. Demetrius must go through the courts if he has a complaint. You must let these men go before something happens that everyone will regret.'

The crowd dispersed and Paul's friends were released. Paul decided it was time to move on.

344 PARTS OF ONE BODY

Paul wrote to the Christians in Corinth while he was in Ephesus.

He had heard that some of the new Christians were jealous of each other and were arguing among themselves. Paul wanted to show them how important it was for them to care about each other and to work together peacefully:

'Christ is like one body that is made of many different parts. We were all baptised so that we are part of that body and we were all given the Holy Spirit.

'Each part of the body has its own special place; each part is important. If each part works and does its job well, the whole body works well, but if any part fails to do its job, the whole body suffers.

'So it's no good if the foot decides it cannot be a part of the body because it is not a hand; and it's no good if the ear decides it cannot be a part of the body because it is not an eye. If the whole body were an eye, it could not hear; if the whole body were an ear, it could not smell.

'In just the same way, one part of the body cannot decide that another part is not important or doesn't belong in the body. The eye cannot tell the hand that it is not needed; the head cannot tell the feet that they are not needed.

'Every one of you is part of the body of Christ. God has given each one gifts to use for the good of everyone else. We all need each other. We suffer together and we are happy together. God has given us each other so that his work can be done.'

345 THE MEANING OF LOVE

Paul tried to explain in the same letter to the Corinthian Christians how God wanted them to behave so that others would know they loved him:

'I may be able to speak many languages; I may even be able to speak the language of angels; but if I cannot love, then all I do is make a loud and horrible noise!

'I may be able to prophesy the future and explain things that others find difficult; I may understand what others cannot know, and have enough faith to move mountains but if I have no love, I am nothing.

'Love is patient and kind. Love is not jealous, or conceited or proud. Love is not rude or selfish or bad tempered. Love doesn't get angry easily and it doesn't bear grudges. Love is generous and kind and forgiving. Love is only happy with the truth. Love always protects, always hopes and keeps on trying. Love never fails.'

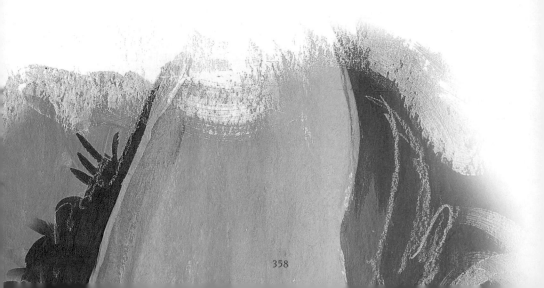

346 PAUL'S SUFFERINGS

While Paul was in Macedonia he wrote again to the Christians in Corinth:

'Let me tell you about some of the things I have done. Let me boast a little about what has happened to me since I first heard Jesus call me to follow him.

'I have worked harder than anyone, been in prison more often, been flogged more severely and been near death more times than I can count. On five occasions the Jews gave me 39 lashes, and on three occasions the Romans beat me with rods. Once I was stoned and three times I was shipwrecked. I have moved from place to place, unable to rest and live a normal life. I have been in danger from floods and from robbers, lived in fear of my fellow Jews and in fear of Gentiles. I have known danger in cities, danger in the countryside and danger at sea. I have sometimes not known whom I could trust. I have worked so hard I thought I could not survive it. I have often gone without sleep or food or water and known what it is to be hungry and thirsty. I have suffered cold and been without shelter or enough clothing.

'To stop me from becoming proud, God also gave me a thorn in the flesh. When I asked God to take it away, he told me that his grace was enough for all my needs. When I am weak, then I ask for his help and strength and he gives it.

'Whatever hardships or difficulties I endure, however weak I feel, I can be happy in them, because I know that in those situations God can make me strong.'

347 GOD'S LOVE

Paul was in Corinth when he wrote a long letter to the new Christians in Rome:

'I believe that anything we suffer now will seem as nothing compared with all the good things that wait for us in the future. Everything in creation is waiting for that day when God will make all things perfect. We are looking forward to that day too, when we will be changed and made perfect.

'We know that in everything God works for the good of the people who love him. And if God is on our side, who can fight against us? Who can separate us from God's love? Can trouble come between us and God? Can hardship or persecution, hunger or poverty, danger or death? No! Jesus loves us, and nothing can separate us from his love: neither death nor life, danger nor trouble, angels nor devils. Nothing that has ever been made can separate us from the love of God—it is ours because Jesus loves us.'

348 A MIRACLE IN TROAS

Paul travelled for a while, sometimes changing his plans when he was warned of plots against his life.

Then, staying briefly in Troas, Paul met one evening with some believers in an upstairs room. They ate together and because Paul knew he would leave the next day, he talked long into the night. He felt there was so much to tell them.

A young man called Eutychus was sitting on the windowsill, listening to Paul. The room was lit by oil lamps and Paul talked on and on. Around midnight Eutychus became so sleepy that he fell out of the window. He died as he hit the ground.

Paul rushed downstairs and threw his arms around Eutychus.

'It's all right!' Paul said to the other believers. 'He's alive!'

The young man's friends were very relieved that Paul had been able to save him. Paul went back upstairs and had something to eat before carrying on talking about Jesus until dawn.

349 DANGER IN JERUSALEM

Paul knew that it was time to go back to Jerusalem. He also knew that it would be dangerous. The Holy Spirit had warned him that prison and hardships awaited him there.

After some time at sea, Paul landed at Caesarea, and stayed for a few days with Philip, the evangelist, and his family. While he was there, a Christian called Agabus came to see Paul. God had given Agabus the gift of prophecy. He took Paul's belt and tied up his own hands and feet with it so that he could not move.

'This is what the Holy Spirit says will happen to the owner of this belt when he goes to Jerusalem,' prophesied Agabus. 'The Jews in Jerusalem will capture him and give him to the Gentiles.'

All his friends were very anxious for Paul's safety. They begged him not to go on any further when they heard this, but Paul would not listen.

'You mustn't cry for me,' he said. 'I am prepared to die in Jerusalem for Jesus, if that's what lies ahead.'

The believers knew that they could not stop him. Paul was determined to go.

'God's will be done,' they said.

Then they prepared to let him leave for Jerusalem.

350 PAUL CAUSES A RIOT

Paul met his friends in Jerusalem and told them about the thousands of people who had become believers in the places where he had travelled. At first they praised God and were happy with Paul, but then they warned him that this very good news would cause problems for him.

They were right. When Paul went to the temple, he was recognised.

'Look!' a group shouted. 'This is the man who tells people to ignore our Jewish customs!'

People rushed into the temple from all directions. They seized him and, dragging him outside the temple area, started to beat him to death. There was such an uproar that Roman troops were sent to stop the riot. As soon as the soldiers rushed into the crowd, the people attacking him stood back.

'Arrest this man,' the Roman commander ordered, 'and bind him in chains.' Then he asked the crowd what Paul had done.

Everyone in the crowd started shouting, but the commander could make no sense of what they were saying.

'Take him to the barracks,' the commander ordered. The crowd became so noisy and violent at this that the soldiers had to carry Paul over the heads of the crowd.

Before he was taken to the barracks, Paul asked the commander if he could speak to the crowd. He then turned to address them. He explained how God had changed him and given him the task of speaking to the Gentiles. This was too much for the crowd.

'Get rid of this man!' they shouted. 'Put him to death!'

351 PLOTS AGAINST PAUL'S LIFE

Paul was taken away. The orders were to flog him with the scourge, a cruel instrument of torture. As they were preparing him, Paul asked whether it was legal to flog a Roman citizen who had not been found guilty of any crime.

The centurion stopped immediately and told his commander that Paul was a Roman citizen. The commander questioned Paul himself and when he found that it was true, he released him.

A plot was then uncovered against Paul—40 Jewish men met secretly and swore they would not eat or drink until Paul was dead.

'Prepare 200 soldiers, 70 horsemen and 200 spearmen,' the commander ordered. 'This man will be taken safely on horseback to Caesarea tonight!'

The commander sent a letter to Governor Felix explaining what had happened. He asked him to judge the case when Paul's accusers arrived there.

352 PAUL ON TRIAL

Five days later, Ananias, the high priest, plus some elders and a lawyer called Tertullus arrived in Caesarea.

'This man is a troublemaker,' Tertullus said to Felix. 'Talk to him yourself and he will not deny what happens wherever he goes!'

Felix gestured to Paul to defend himself.

'I had been in Jerusalem for only twelve days before I was taken prisoner,' Paul said. 'I have been guilty of nothing. I caused no riot or disturbance. I did not go round with a crowd causing trouble. I am a Christian, a follower of what is called here "the Way", and I know that I have offended some because I believe in life after death.'

Felix had heard of 'the Way' and adjourned the case. He kept Paul under guard but made sure his friends were allowed to see him and make him comfortable. Felix and his wife Drusilla even met Paul and listened to him as he talked about Jesus.

Felix waited. He hoped that Paul would offer him a bribe to release him, but after two years, Paul was still in prison.

Then a new governor took over. When Porcius Festus arrived, Paul's enemies tried to set a date for a new trial in Jerusalem so they could arrange to kill Paul on the journey there.

Festus refused. Instead he went with the Jewish elders to Caesarea and the new trial began. Still nothing could be proved.

'I have broken no Jewish law; I have not broken Emperor Caesar's law,' insisted Paul. 'I am a Roman citizen and I have the right to appeal to Caesar.'

Festus talked with his council.

'You have appealed to Caesar,' he said. 'We have wasted enough time. Now, Paul, you will go to Rome!'

353 THE SHIPWRECK

Paul was finally on his way to Rome. A centurion called Julius took charge of Paul and they set sail for Italy, but the winds were against them, as it was nearly the time of the autumn storms. When they reached the island of Crete, Paul tried to warn Julius that lives could be lost but Julius would not listen.

Soon they were hit by a hurricane-force wind. The sailors struggled to keep the ship under control, and suffered so much damage they had to throw some of the cargo overboard. Then dense clouds made navigation impossible. The ship was driven aimlessly by wind and waves.

An angel appeared to Paul one night and told him not to be afraid as God would keep all on the ship safe.

So Paul told the rest of the ship's passengers that the ship would be lost but they would be saved. He urged them all to eat and so to save their strength.

There were 276 people on board the ship. When daylight came, they saw land but the ship ran aground and broke up. The soldiers wanted to kill the prisoners to stop them from escaping but Julius prevented them. So everyone made their way to land, either by swimming or by clinging to pieces of the wreckage.

They had landed on the island of Malta.

354 MIRACLES ON THE ISLAND OF MALTA

Rain was falling heavily and it was cold. The people who lived on the island rushed to the beach and made a fire. They helped the shipwrecked men to safety.

As Paul gathered some wood to add to the fire, a snake slithered out and sank its fangs into his hand. The islanders who saw the snake whispered among themselves.

'This man has escaped from the sea to be killed by a snake bite. He must be a murderer!'

Paul shook off the snake and did not seem to be in pain. They watched and waited but Paul did not become ill or die.

The chief official in Malta was a man named Publius. He invited everyone to his home and made them welcome for three days.

During this time, Paul found that Publius' father was ill. He lay in bed, hot and feverish and suffering from dysentery. Paul went and prayed with him and the man was healed. After that, many people on the island came to Paul with their illnesses and Paul healed them all.

When it was safe to resume their journey by sea once more, the people on the island made sure that they had all the supplies they needed. They sailed on an Alexandrian ship to Rome.

355 A PRISONER IN ROME

Paul arrived safely in Italy. He was placed under house arrest in Rome but was otherwise allowed to live freely.

First he called together the leaders of the Jewish population there. He explained to them why he had been sent there and tried again to help them see that Jesus was the one they had been waiting for. Some among them believed him; others were not convinced.

Paul now knew that his job was to reach the Gentiles in Rome with his message. For two years he welcomed people to his rented house and taught them all he knew about Jesus. Many believed what he had to say and were baptised. Paul also wrote many letters to the Christians he had met over the years, helping them in their Christian faith and teaching them when there were things they did not understand.

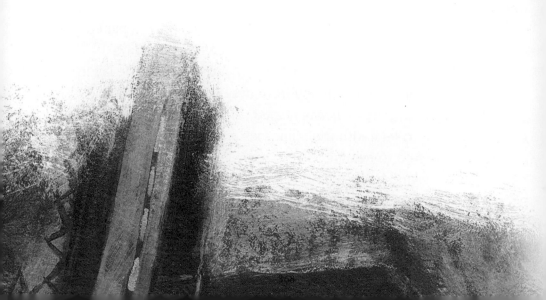

356 GOD'S ARMOUR

While he was a prisoner in Rome, Paul wrote to the Christians in Ephesus:

'Since you are God's children, you must try to be like him. Live your lives controlled by love, not hate, just as Jesus himself gave up his life because he loved us.

'Don't be afraid to stand up against what is wrong. Be strong and remember that he will look after you and give you power. Wear God's armour so that you will be safe: wear truth like a belt around your waist; cover your heart with the breastplate of righteousness; wear shoes ready to tell other people about the good news of Jesus; carry faith as your shield against all attacks; accept as a helmet the salvation which Jesus bought with his life; and use God's word as a sword.'

357 GOD'S FRIENDS

One day a slave called Onesimus visited Paul in his house in Rome.
Onesimus had run away from his master, but when he listened to all
that Paul told him about Jesus, he became a Christian and helped Paul
in his work.

Onesimus went with Tychicus to take a letter from Paul and his
friend Timothy to the Christians in Colossae:

'Jesus is the human likeness of the invisible God. He existed before
all things were created and is now the head of the church. It was
because of the sacrifice Jesus made when he died on the cross that
God could forgive sin and make peace with his people.

'Once you were far away from God; you were his enemies because of
the evil things you thought and said and did. Now, because Jesus died
on the cross, God has made you his friends.'

358 THE RUNAWAY SLAVE

Onesimus still belonged to his master, Philemon, who was a leader in the church at Colossae. Onesimus had become a good friend while Paul was a prisoner, but he knew he could not let Onesimus stay in Rome. Paul therefore wrote a letter for Onesimus to take back with him to Philemon:

'My dear friend Philemon, I have heard so much about your love for God and for other people. Now I need to ask you to do something for me, something I am sure you would want to do anyway. Onesimus was wrong to leave you and I am sending him back. While he was away, he has become a Christian and as such is now not only your slave but also your brother. I would have loved him to stay and work with me, but I wanted your agreement first.

'Please welcome him back as you would welcome me into your home. If he owes you anything, I will pay it back. I hope to be able to visit you soon. Please get the guestroom ready for me.'

359 LIVING LIKE JESUS

The Christians at Philippi also received a letter from Paul while he was in Rome:

'What is life? For me, it is to love and serve Jesus, to do what he wants me to do. Yet if I die, that too is good, because then I will be with Jesus always. I cannot choose which is better: life or death!

'Make sure you live in a way that pleases God and shows other people that you belong to him. Don't be selfish or conceited, but think of others as better than yourself. Put other people first. Think about how Jesus treated other people and try to be like him.

'Jesus had the nature of God himself, yet he didn't behave as though he was above anyone or more important than the people he had come to serve. Instead he came to earth as a man and acted as a servant. He allowed himself to be betrayed and humiliated, beaten and then unjustly executed as if he were a criminal. Jesus obeyed God and put others first. So God has rewarded him and has given him the highest position in heaven and earth. One day, when people hear the name of Jesus, the whole world will bow down and call him Lord.

'So, there is nothing I want more than to know Jesus and share in his sufferings, even if I die, because then I will also know his resurrection and eternal life. This is my aim in life: to follow Jesus to the end.'

360 THE END OF TIME

Paul was not the only apostle to write letters to encourage other Christians. Peter wrote two letters:

'Some of you are suffering and going through difficult times because you are now Christians. Be happy that you are sharing in what Jesus suffered for you, but tell God all about your troubles because he cares about you.

'The time will come when everyone will know that God is king. Remember that God is outside time. For him one day is like a thousand years. It may be tomorrow; it may be after we have died. God is patient and he wants everyone to repent and know him; God wants no one to perish without knowing about his love.

'When that day comes, it will creep up on us. The earth as we know it will come to an end. There will be no warning. We must therefore live our lives so that we will not be ashamed when it happens. We must be ready for God to come in glory, and we can look forward to a new heaven and a new earth.'

361 JESUS, THE HIGH PRIEST

Another long letter was written to help Jewish Christians.

'God's word is living and active, sharper than any sword, helping us to judge between right and wrong. We can hide nothing from God. We do not need to be afraid, because we have a special high priest, Jesus, God's Son, who understands our human nature and sympathises with our weaknesses, though he did not sin. We can come to God with confidence and know that we will receive his mercy and that he will help us in our need.

'We are saved by God because we have faith. Faith is being sure of what we hope for, certain of what we do not see. We are part of a huge number of others who had faith before us, among them Abel, Enoch and Noah; Abraham, Isaac, Jacob and Joseph; Moses and the people with Joshua including Rahab; all the faithful prophets and kings of Israel. So, with them, we must set out on the race God has set before us, throwing off all the sins that get in our way, and looking at Jesus, who suffered so much for us. Be strong, and don't be discouraged.'

362 LOVE ONE ANOTHER

John, one of Jesus' special friends, wrote at least three letters to the Christians in new churches.

'God is light and in him there is no darkness. We must live in that light too, and to do this we must confess our sins and not try to hide them or pretend we haven't sinned at all. If we confess our sins and tell God we are sorry, then he will forgive us.

'Loving God means loving other people. It is wrong to hate someone else. If we hate someone, we sin and we need to confess that sin. God's love is so great that he calls us his children! Let's behave as if we are his children and love the other members of his family.

'We know what real love is by looking at Jesus. He gave up his life for us. We should be prepared to do that for someone else. If we have enough to eat and drink and a home to live in and we know people who are starving or in any kind of need and we ignore them, then how can we say God's love is in us? Don't just talk about God's love! Show what it means by sharing what you have with people in need.

'We love other people because God first loved us. God is love. Now we must show that love to the people of the world by loving them.'

363 JOHN'S VISION

When John was an old man, he was sent to live in exile on the island of Patmos.

One day, the Holy Spirit revealed strange things to John and told him to write them down on a scroll and send them to the Christians in Ephesus, Smyrna, Pergamum, Thyatira, Sardis, Philadelphia and Laodicea.

John looked to see who it was who was speaking to him and was amazed to see Jesus, not as he remembered him from when they worked together in Galilee, but shining like the sun, God in all his glory.

The sight was so awesome that John fell at Jesus' feet. Then Jesus touched John's head gently and spoke:

'Do not be afraid, John,' he said. 'I am the first and the last, the Living One. I was dead, but look, I am alive now and I will live for ever and ever.'

364 THE REVELATION OF GOD

John wrote down all that Jesus told him to say to the people in the seven churches. Then he looked up and saw a door opening into heaven.

'Come here!' said the voice that John had first heard. 'I will show you what will happen in the future.'

John no longer felt as if his feet were on the ground, but he saw everything clearly.

He saw a magnificent throne surrounded by an emerald green rainbow with someone sitting on it, who seemed to shine like colourful precious stones. There were 24 other thrones and on each one there was someone dressed in white, wearing a golden crown.

The throne in the middle was God's throne and it flashed with light, and there was a sound like thunder. In front of it was a sparkling crystal sea.

Around the throne were four strange creatures, covered with eyes. They were like a lion, an ox, a man and an eagle, yet they each had six wings.

'Holy, holy, holy God, who was, and is, and is to come,' they sang continually.

The 24 people fell down before God, and worshipped him.

'You are worthy to receive glory and honour and power. You created everything, and everything lives and breathes because of you,' they said.

365 A NEW HEAVEN AND A NEW EARTH

John saw thousands upon thousands of people from all over the world, dressed in white, holding palm branches in their hands. They stood before God's throne, which was surrounded by angels and the four strange creatures, all worshipping him. A man came from one of the thrones.

'These people are those who have suffered,' he told John. 'They have been saved because of the blood shed by Jesus.'

Later, John saw that the earth had gone, and that there was a new heaven and a new earth. He saw a wonderful new city.

'Now God will live with his people. There will be no more pain or death, no more sadness or crying. God will wipe every tear from their eyes,' God said. 'Anyone who comes to me will drink and never be thirsty again. I will be his God and he will be my child.'

Then an angel showed John the beautiful new city, with the water of life flowing in a sparkling river over which grew the tree of life which brought healing and freedom to people of every nation.

Then Jesus spoke: 'I am coming soon! I am the first and the last, the beginning and the end. Anyone who comes to me will be forgiven, and those who are forgiven will be happy and will live in the city and enjoy life. Anyone who wants to can come and drink freely from the water of life.

'I am coming soon!'

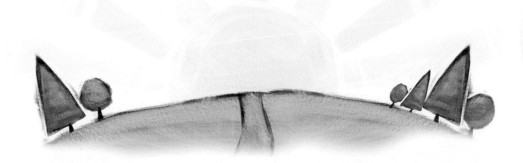